Stress
and the
Teaching Profession

Stress
and the
Teaching Profession

by
Sheldon F. Greenberg, Ph.D.

·P·A·U·L·H·
BROOKES
PUBLISHING C<u>O</u>

Baltimore • London

Paul H. Brookes Publishing Co.
Post Office Box 10624
Baltimore, Maryland 21204 9/9/

Typeset by The Composing Room of Michigan (Grand Rapids).
Manufactured in the United States of America by
The Maple Press Company, York, Pennsylvania.

Library of Congress Cataloging in Publication Data
Greenberg, Sheldon F., 1948–
    Stress and the teaching profession.

    Bibliography: p.
    Includes index.
    1. Teachers—Job stress.   I. Title.
LB2840.2.G74   1984   371.1′001′9   84-6379
ISBN 0-933716-39-7

Contents

Preface

It is usually not until much later in their lives that most people reflect on teachers they had and the lessons they learned that carried forth into their own lives. They remember that one special teacher who took extra time to make a point or correct a weakness, the one who went beyond what was required and gave more. For some people, the extra effort resulted in greater self-confidence. It may have been advice on how to cope with a difficult situation at home, or it may have simply been some love and caring.

Unfortunately, most people recall their special teachers too late to go back and extend their gratitude. At the time they were students, their thoughts were simply on getting good grades, getting through the school year, staying out of trouble, or planning their after-school social events. Few gave thought to the trials and anxieties of their teachers.

However, these trials and anxieties are part of each teacher's everyday routine. Daily activities may cause physical, mental, and emotional strain as the educator works to impart knowledge and skills to students of varying learning levels, interests, and personalities. These instructors who devote themselves to educating others, whether they be elementary school teachers, college professors, or school administrators, may easily succumb to the negative effects of job-related stress.

In addition to facing the strains that accompany the effective education of others, teachers today are faced with open criticism from the media and government. They hear and read that the educational system is not working well enough, that American youth are not being as well educated as those in some other nations, or that there should be a crackdown on teacher evaluation systems. Such attention has created new pressures on teachers to perform.

This text addresses many of the common and new stresses and strains faced by educators every day. It outlines, in nontechnical language, the nature of stress . . . what it is, how it works, how to recognize its harmful effects, and what to do to control and reduce it. Specific issues within the educational system are addressed, too. Teacher evaluation systems, turnover rate, lack of resources, inconsistencies in policies and procedures, and parental influence are just a few. The causes of stress in education are both numerous and varied. In addition, this text focuses on practical ways in which educators can reduce and control the stress they experience. Simple techniques ranging from modifying diet or taking brief walks can be implemented with a minimum of effort at the educator's leisure. Others, such as working within the framework of the educator's labor organization or professional association, are more complex.

The aim of the text is to provide educators with a better understanding of the specific nature of stress in the field and how it can be overcome. The educator who understands and applies this will, most likely, enjoy a longer, more rewarding career. Attitudes toward students, peers, and administrators improve when stress is reduced. Attitudes toward self, family, and relationships also improve.

This text is for educators who care about their profession and themselves. Someone once said that a teacher cannot burn out unless he or she is first "on fire." *Stress and the Teaching Profession* is for educators who have been or remain "on fire" about the field and who either want to avoid succumbing to job stress or want to be rekindled.

Society is awakening rapidly to the harmful impact of too much stress on the individual. The turnover rate in education gives cause to look more closely at the field to determine why so many people who have devoted years of study to learn their trade resign to enter other professions. This text is intended for good teachers who care and who want to enjoy their career.

Dedication

This book is dedicated to the following people, with love and lifelong devotion. They have made my life rich and full.

My brothers and their wives: Mark and Terry, Glenn and Elaine, Yale and Reggie, and Morris, for their love and the wonderful closeness we share.

Dr. McCay Vernon, Dr. David Denton, and Dr. Alfred J. Smith, Jr., for their guidance, caring, and inspiration.

The Vanek family: Charles, Doris, Mike, and Rob, for their friendship, support, and warmth.

Chris Dawson, my youngest friend, for his hugs and for being very special to me.

S. G.

Stress
and the
Teaching Profession

Chapter 1

Introduction

The headline in the newspaper article read, "More Teachers Are Wiping the Chalk Dust Off Their Fingers Forever" (Kidder, 1979). The article began by citing a sign in the teachers' lounge of a Wichita, Kansas, high school that said, "Would the last one resigning please turn out the lights?" It went on to address the increasingly high turnover rate among experienced educators (Kidder, 1979).

Another headline, this one in an educational journal, read, "Is Teaching Hazardous to Your Health?" The article summarized a survey conducted by *Instructor* magazine, a professional publication in the field of elementary education. The survey pointed out that while a wealth of data exists on employee health and job stress in most professions, very little exists that deals specifically with education (Landsmann, 1978). The publication surveyed its readers, receiving 9,000 responses. Asked about days off due to illness, three-fourths of the readers stated that they had missed days from work due to stress or tension. Over one-third noted that they had called in sick because of fatigue or nervous strain. Eighty-four percent of the responding readers stated that they believed there are distinct health hazards in teaching. The majority cited stress as the major force affecting their health (Landsmann, 1978).

Stress is not a new phenomenon in education. Nor is it new to other fields and occupations. Dr. Hans Selye, president of the International Institute of Stress in Montreal, and one of the leaders in stress research, was conducting experiments and writing journal articles on the topic of stress in education more than 40 years ago. In 1974, the president of the Blue Cross and Blue Shield Associations referred to stress as "one of the most common problems . . . that attacks all of us, at all ages" (McNerney, 1974).

WHAT IS STRESS?

The definitions of stress are many and varied, ranging from simple one-word statements such as "tension" or "pressure," to complex medical explanations

1

for the physiological responses of the human body to certain stimuli. McNerney defines it as the "body's physical, mental, and chemical reactions to circumstances that frighten, excite, confuse, endanger, or irritate" (McNerney, 1974). It has also been defined as an external, noxious force that exerts undesirable and unpleasant effects on an individual (Graham-Bonnalie, 1972). Selye defines stress simply as "the nonspecific response of the body to any demand made on it" (Selye, 1976). He notes that some stress is not only good but that it is essential to daily living. He concludes that it is impossible for a person to completely avoid stress. It exists everywhere. The total absence of stress is achieved only in death.

In sum, stress is the *physical, mental, or emotional reaction resulting from an individual's response to environmental tensions, conflicts, pressures, and other stimuli.* It is much more than nervous anxiety and feelings of tension and tightness, as many people believe. A person's reaction to stress may be clearly visible to both the individual and to those with whom he or she spends time. The reaction may also be subtle, with the individual unaware of the effects of stress until an illness or disorder surfaces.

Stress causes a reaction in the human body. The stress may be negative, the result of a difficult day or a confrontation with a student. It may also be positive, resulting from an extended vacation or birthday celebration. In either case, it will affect the cardiovascular, digestive, and musculoskeletal systems (Greenberg & Valletutti, 1980).

An action or stimulus creating stress is a *stressor*. A person's reactions to stressors and the effects of stressors may have impact on daily functioning to such a degree that coping with everyday activities becomes impossible. Another person may react in such a way that accomplishments are increased and challenges of daily living are met successfully. Such a person will usually exclaim, "I work best under pressure."

Every person, whether a teacher, firefighter, homemaker, or engineer, is exposed to numerous stressors every day. Some stressors are very general, while others are specific. Specific stressors, for example, may include going outdoors into the heat or cold, eating a lunch that is too big or small, or having to wait in line at a checkout counter. Others may include personal finances, sexual relationships, children, professional advancement and promotional opportunity, rush hour traffic, supervisory evaluations, mowing the lawn, and going to dinner with relatives.

Examples of general stressors may include the philosophical changes occurring within the field of education, or exposure to occupational controversy. The American public school teacher, for example, once a symbol of constancy and stability, has become a controversial figure. Such controversy is usually accompanied by increased stress for the practitioner.

The changes that have taken place in education are many and varied. Once a field that faced few challenges from outsiders, education has now grown into a favorite target of politicians, special interest groups, unions, parents, and others. Where the task of developing curricula and designing instructional techniques was once the responsibility of the classroom teacher, it has now become the responsibility of administration. Federal grant funds, which at one time seemed unlimited, have declined, placing school systems and colleges in serious fiscal constraints. New emphasis has been put on planning and accountability. And, in a field that rarely experienced labor difficulties, labor strikes and the threat of strikes have become more common.

STRESS AND THE HELPING PROFESSIONS

In 1978, Brown University conducted a study that confirmed a higher incidence of stress-related illnesses among people whose jobs require that they bear significant responsibility for the well-being of others (Anderson, 1978). People in human service fields experience higher incidents of heart attack, diabetes, and circulatory system disorders, as well as marital problems, job dissatisfaction, and more.

Teachers, physicians, nurses, social workers, firefighters, attorneys, clergymen and -women, counselors, police officers, and other practitioners who have made a commitment to caring for others are regularly exposed to an environment that may exacerbate the negative effects of stress on the individual (Greenberg & Valletutti, 1980).

Human service workers become more deeply involved in the lives of their clients, patients, students, and congregants. They get to know those they serve and often develop emotional ties to them. They get to know their personalities, background, families, and personal problems and aspirations. Workers in these fields generally have some power or authority over the activities of those they serve. This is a significant responsibility, taken quite seriously by most practitioners.

Many human service workers are regularly exposed to human grief, personal problems, and human difficulties. They see others who are unable to cope with daily functions that many people view as routine. They've committed themselves to working with others regardless of the physical, mental, and emotional weaknesses these people may display. The hours of most human service workers are long and irregular. Their commitment to put in unusual hours often goes unnoticed. Compensation for the hours worked above the standard work week rarely exists.

The activities performed by most people in the human service or helping professions are varied and, often, may be unrelated to their job description. For example, a teacher may regularly tend to the social, health, or familial needs of students. A physician may have to double as a counselor. A police officer may have to function in the role of arbitrator.

Most human service workers must rely on the services and resources of others in order to perform their assigned tasks successfully. They must maintain a thorough working knowledge of these available services and resources in order to make rapid and effective referral. Yet, the service and resource agencies may not respond in a timely manner or with such sufficiency as required to meet presented needs.

Generally, members of the helping professions are required by their systems to serve too many people, with too few resources. Elementary school teachers continue to teach classes of 35, 40, or 45 students in many parts of the United States. This is contrary to the private enterprise system in which resources and staffing increase in conjunction with demand for the product being offered.

While there are many similarities among the human service fields, each has its unique characteristics, goals, clientele, and stressors. Teachers, for example, have been described as being caught in a network of paradoxes unique to the field of education.

> Education is said to be at the very heart of the nation's culture, but teachers lack prestige. Schools, it's said, have played a major role in bringing about this nation's affluence, yet many schools and most teachers are largely excluded from that prosperity. Teachers form the largest occupational block in the country, but they have none of the political power of the farm block, which they've supplanted in terms of sheer numbers. . . . When teachers are interviewed about themselves and their world, it's these self-contradictions and other conflicts that come through strongly (Brenton, 1970).

Stress in Education

It is difficult to determine which segment of the educational system is most frequently subject to the negative effects of stress. Is a classroom teacher in an elementary school subject to greater stress than a high school or college administrator? Does the teacher in a private school work in a better environment than a teacher in a public school?

While every educator experiences strain and tension unique to his or her specific assignment, many stressors are shared by everyone in the field. For example, no educator, whether in a preschool, higher education, or individual tutorial environment, can escape the pressures of declining budgets and increased scrutiny by the media and the public. Thus, there are many reasons for providing stress awareness and management information to educators at every level and within every segment of the educational system. There is no immunity from the negative effects of stress. Its impact is felt in every corner of the education community.

Teachers are leaving their profession at an increased rate. In one poll, one-third of the teachers questioned said that they would not enter the field if they had an opportunity to choose again. Only 60% of those polled said that they planned to teach until they could retire (Truch, 1980).

Many young teachers leave the field of education during their first 5 years on the job. Because of their age, they appear professionally attractive to business and industry, and are able to begin a new career. They've realized early that they are dissatisfied and do not want to make a commitment to a 25- or 30-year career.

On the other hand, older teachers are retiring earlier. They are taking 20-year retirements early rather than continuing for 25 or 30 years, even though the extended career would result in substantial increases in retirement income. In England, death among male teachers who are near retirement age has doubled during the past 10 years. The number of teachers who qualify for medical pensions has tripled. One recent study indicated that the life expectancy of a teacher is 4 years lower than the national average (Truch, 1980).

In surveys, 90% of all teachers questioned indicated that they felt some stress. About 95% of the teachers indicated the need for stress-management courses. The results of other surveys indicate that teaching may be the third most stressful of all occupations, following air traffic controllers and surgeons (Truch, 1980).

In the book, *Teacher and Child,* Ginott (1975) recorded the conversation of a group of teachers discussing their disillusionment with the educational system and how they were going to deal with their feelings. Some of their statements were:

After one year of experience, I've decided I am not fit for my job. I came to teaching full of love and fantasy. Now, the illusions have evaporated and the love has gone. Teaching is not a profession. It's slow murder, death in daily installments.

I am so sad I could cry. I am disappointed and disenchanted, because I expected so much.

If you don't take it to heart, it's not that bad . . . I know the system and have no false hopes. It's a racket. I don't like it but I don't fight it. I live with it and get all I can from it.

Every day I come to school full of energy. I return home half dead. The noise drives me mad.

I want to educate children to work for peace. The irony is that I am continuously embroiled in battles with them. It just doesn't make sense to me.

I look back in anger at the last year—the wasted time, the listless hours, the long conferences, the futile talks. Our principal loves vagueness and adores ambiguity. He delays decisions and postpones life.

I became aware that college failed to prepare me for my job. Teaching children takes at least as much skill as flying a jet. In college they taught us to drive a tractor, while telling us it was a jet. No wonder we crash every time we try to take off.

The whole system of education is built on distrust. The teacher distrusts the students. The principal distrusts the teachers. The superintendent suspects the principals, and the school board is wary of the superintendent (Ginott, 1975).

Of course, not every teacher is disillusioned and discontented. Many work well within the system, doing their part to improve weaknesses and build on strengths, all for the benefit of their students. They, too, experience the stresses inherent in education. While they maintain a consistently healthy attitude toward their profession and their schools, they experience the strains and tensions of declining budgets, overworked support systems, and demanding, disgruntled parents.

THE NEED TO STUDY STRESS:
MANAGEMENT AND COPING TECHNIQUES

Whether induced by problems that exist within the school system or by personal tensions resulting from home and family, stress and its negative effects interfere with peace and harmony in daily functioning. The stresses and strains of teaching a lesson and managing a classroom are, in themselves, voluminous. Compounding them are the stresses and strains related to administration, supervision, marriage, a home, finances, and more.

Generally, gaining an awareness of the causes and symptoms of stress, and understanding techniques for coping with it, will prepare an educator for warding off many stress-related illnesses. The individual educator benefits from a more comfortable work environment, a more pleasant home and family situation, and an improved self-concept. In turn, the students and the school system gain.

The nature of education requires that maximum attention be given to the well-being of students. This often means that the teacher cannot spend appropriate time attending to his or her own well-being. So much of the educator's energy is expended in treating and coping with the mental, physical, and emotional ills of others that little is left for personal care and development beyond the basic necessities. The educator's own well-being receives scant attention. The same is true for other human service professionals. Like the doctor whose daughter is always sick, or the police officer whose son is in trouble with the law, members of the human service fields often become candidates for their own services (Greenberg & Valletutti, 1980).

Regarding the impact of stress on all people, Dr. Thomas H. Budzynski, of the Biofeedback Institute in Denver, stated that "although stress is a relatively new concept in our culture, most of us will die of disorders related to our inability to cope successfully with it" (Budzynski & Stoyva, 1971). Most members of the helping professions who do not associate the emotional and physical problems occurring in their jobs with stress and who continually make the care of self a second or third priority, dramatically increase their chances of succumbing to stress-related disorders (Greenberg & Valletutti, 1980).

In addition to not being aware of the impact of stress and not taking the time to care for self, most people are unaware of the cumulative effects stress can have on a person. Selye once called stress "the speedometer of life," noting that it is the "sum of all the wear and tear caused by any kind of vital reaction throughout the body at one time" (1976). He noted:

> Many people believe that, after they have exposed themselves to very stressful activities, a rest can restore them to where they were before. This is false. Experi-

ments on animals have clearly shown that each exposure leaves an indelible scar, in that it uses up reserves of adaptability which cannot be replaced. It is true that immediately after some harassing experience, rest can restore us almost to the original level of fitness by removing fatigue. But the emphasis is on the word "almost." Since we constantly go through periods of stress and rest during life, just a little deficit of adaptation energy every day adds up . . . it adds up to what we call aging (Selye, 1976).

Ignoring stress and the illnesses and disorders often associated with it has been termed a mild and slow form of suicide (Greenberg & Valletutti, 1980). Stress builds over time, sometimes slowly and sometimes rapidly. The mind, emotions, and body, with their many adaptive processes, cope with the stress and hold it in place, much the same as a balloon holds air. If allowed to build, the stress will lead to such strain that, like an overinflated balloon, it will cause a sudden and negative shock to the system. Selye stated, "More and more people are killed by disease producers which cannot be eliminated by the methods of classic medicine. An ever-increasing proportion of the human population dies from the so-called wear-and-tear diseases, which are primarily due to stress" (Selye, 1976).

The need for educators to study stress-management techniques and to apply them to their daily routines is great. Their vulnerability to the negative effects of stress grows with every change in the educational system. Their dedication to serving others, the responsibility they assume for the care and success of their students, long work hours, low pay, lack of recognition, and lack of advancement opportunities add to their vulnerability. More than most others, educators must take an active, responsible role in ensuring their own personal health and well-being. Inherent in this is the study and application of stress management.

Destroying Some Myths

In order to gain a useful understanding of what stress is and how it affects the body, mind, and emotions, it is important to dispel some of the most commonly accepted myths surrounding it. Misconceptions about stress have developed and been accepted over the years, due in part to the small amount of research and concrete information available on it. The study of stress is a relatively new endeavor and it will take many more years of research before the old misconceptions fade away.

All Stress Is Bad The most common misconception about stress is that it is always harmful and that its effects are always negative. A multibillion dollar industry of medications, relaxation devices, therapy, and spas has been built on this misconception, which while effective in dealing with stress, also supports this misconception. Selye (1976) and others have called stress the "spice of life" and have shown that it is impossible to avoid it in daily life. Stress exists in good, pleasant situations as well as in bad ones. A vacation, new car, new home, new child, and promotions are all stressful to some degree, yet all are rewarding.

For some people, stress in a negative environment is not harmful. For example, a teacher who faces a classroom of disruptive students on a daily basis is faced with a negative situation. Yet, for that teacher, the situation may offer a challenge. His or her potential may be taxed and performance may, in fact, exceed the norm. In this case, the stress of the situation has motivated the individual to heightened achievement.

Stress May Be Reduced or Eliminated with Tranquilizers and Drugs   No drug or tranquilizer, whether it be a narcotic prescribed by a physician or a glass of scotch whiskey at the end of the day, is capable of eliminating stress. Instead, the intake of tranquilizers and drugs simply masks the effects or symptoms of stress. Most physicians believe that the effects of such attempts to mask stress are harmful since the stress continues to exist once the effects of the drug have worn off.

Stress Should Be Avoided   Negative stress should be avoided. However, since some stress exists in almost every activity a person faces, avoiding it completely becomes an impossibility. Many negative stressors such as a weak supervisor, an illness, or a financial problem, cannot be avoided. To attempt to do so would be a futile effort.

By Working Less, a Person May Avoid Stress   Work does not cause stress. Stress on the job is often the result of how a person reacts to activities and people within the work environment. While enjoying leisure time is one way to reduce the negative effects of stress for some, many people approach their nonwork time in a stressful manner, scheduling more home or hobby activities than can be reasonably handled in a given period of time. Most researchers in the area of stress management place emphasis on the quality of work and leisure time rather than the quantity.

Stress Only Affects Adults   Many adults envy the freedom from stress enjoyed by children. Yet, children experience stress in much the same way as adults. Their stressors are different and may range from losing a favorite toy to having to go to bed at a specific time. Whatever the cause, the stress experienced by young children is real. For teenagers, focusing on dating, wearing fashionable apparel, and achieving satisfactory grades may cause insurmountable stress. The techniques young people use to cope with stress are generally different from those used by adults, but the degree of stress and many of its effects are the same.

Administrators and Supervisors Experience a Greater Degree of Stress Than Classroom Teachers   There is no correlation between the degree of stress experienced by an individual in a nonsupervisory position within an organization and that experienced by supervisors, administrators, and other managers working in the same place of business. In a study of 270,000 men by Cornell University Medical College, it was determined that those who had risen to executive positions had a lower rate of heart attack than those in first-level positions (McQuade & Aikman, 1979).

Stress Cannot Be Defeated   Many people accept the negative effects of stress as a fact of life and believe that little can be done to control or reduce it.

Research does not support this belief. Techniques for managing stress and reducing its negative effects can be learned and applied to daily living with great success by almost everyone. These techniques can serve to reduce high blood pressure, relax muscular tension, set the mind at ease, and provide vigor in the place of fatigue. The negative effects of stress may, in fact, be controlled.

Succumbing to the Negative Effects of Stress Is a Sign of Weakness While considerable attention has been given to the impact of stress on the average person, there are many people who believe that an inability to cor ᷄ with a stress-related illness is a sign of weakness. The truth is that even the most dedicated, hard-working, professionally strong teachers succumb to heart attacks, ulcers, migraine headaches, and more. Succumbing to stress-related illnesses and disorders is not a sign of weakness in the individual. Personal strengths and weaknesses are but a small part of the variables that may contribute to distress.

The number of myths surrounding the subject of stress and its management are many. They may be based on psychological denial or rooted in attitudes developed in youth. They may also be based on lack of knowledge or misunderstanding of the knowledge that exists. Whatever the cause, the myths and misunderstandings about stress often prevent people from trying to manage it and, subsequently, enjoying a full and rewarding life.

Assuming Responsibility and Taking the Initiative

The first, and probably the most important, step in managing stress and its harmful effects is recognizing that it exists and that the individual is fully capable of managing it. Too often, the responsibility or blame for the stress in a person's life is placed on someone or something else. Common targets of blame for a teacher, for example, are the school system, the principal, other teachers, students, parents, a spouse, finances, and a lack of promotional opportunity. While each of these may, in fact, be causes of stress to the teacher, casting blame does little to reduce the backaches, indigestion, spastic colon, fatigue, and nervous tension.

The individual educator, by assuming responsibility for his or her own well-being and by taking the initiative to develop a personal stress-management plan, can defeat some of the negative effects of stress. Many of the initiatives are simple and may be applied to daily living comfortably. Others require changes in attitude and life-style, working to defeat old habits and create new ones. Still others require difficult decision making and may include the restructuring of life goals.

For the educator who waits for the school system or principal to correct all of his or her professional ills, there will be little accomplished in the reduction of stress. While some responsibility rests with the system and its administration to ensure a comfortable work environment, the responsibility for management of stress on the job must be shared jointly with the individual practitioner.

Similarly, the management of stress as it relates to home, family, and social life is a joint process. The "me—them" syndrome, in which "me" is always right and "them" is always at fault, is often the cause for failure to reduce and control stress. Cooperation and teamwork are, conversely, at the foundation of success. The cooperative, teamwork approach to stress management will only evolve when the individual has demonstrated that he or she is willing to assume responsibility and take some initiative in combating the stresses and strains that tend to make life difficult.

SUMMARY

Educating others is a complex and stressful task. It requires skill, patience, mental and physical fitness, and more. Yet, educators are among the most frequently criticized and underpaid practitioners among the human service fields. They are exposed to negative stressors on a daily basis, including increased demands for service in the face of declining fiscal and operational support.

As a result of the stresses and strains inherent in the education of others, teachers experience a high degree of job dissatisfaction, burnout, a high rate of turnover, and a high rate of physical and mental illness. This has weakened the educational system in a variety of ways.

However, stress can be understood and managed. Gaining an awareness of stress-management techniques and applying them to daily activities, both in the educational setting and at home, will not eliminate all of the causes of stress and strain, but can significantly and permanently reduce its negative effects. Subsequently, the teacher or educational administrator may gain an improved health and mental attitude, thereby improving his or her work, family, and social environment.

The individual educator must assume responsibility for the management of stress and must initiate activities to control and reduce it. This may ultimately result in greater involvement by the school system, administrators, family, and friends, to make those changes or implement those programs necessary to an effective stress-management program. Each educator should strive to develop a personal, lifelong stress-management plan. The plan should be designed to reduce and manage stress on both an immediate and long-term basis. It is toward this end that the following chapters are directed.

REFERENCES

Anderson, R. A. *Stress power: How to turn tension into energy.* New York: Human Services Press, 1978.

Brenton, M. *What's happened to teacher?* New York: Coward-McCann, Inc., 1970.

Budzynski, T. H., & Stoyva, J. *Biofeedback techniques in behavior therapy and autogenic training.* Unpublished manuscript, 1971.

Ginott, H. G. *Teacher and child.* New York: Avon Books, 1975.

Graham-Bonnalie, F. E. *The doctor's guide to living with stress.* New York: Drake Publishers, 1972.

Greenberg, S. F., & Valletutti, P. J. *Stress and the helping professions.* Baltimore: Paul H. Brookes Publishing Co., 1980.

Kidder, R. M. More Teachers Are Wiping The Chalk Dust Off Their Hands Forever. *The Sun* (Baltimore), September 9, 1979, Trend Section, p. 10.

Landsmann, L. Is teaching hazardous to your health? *Today's Education,* 1978, April–May, 49–50.

McNerney, W. J. Learning to live successfully in today's world. *Stress: Blueprint For Health.* Chicago: Blue Cross Association, 1974.

McQuade, W., & Aikman, A. *Stress* (4th ed.). New York: E. P. Dutton & Co., 1979.

Selye, H. *The stress of life.* New York: McGraw-Hill Book Co., 1976.

Truch, S. *Teacher burnout.* Novato, CA: Academic Therapy Publications, 1980.

Chapter 2

Expectation
vs. Reality
The Origin of a Teacher's Stress

Stress evolves in many ways. It may be suddenly thrust upon a teacher (in the form of a student who becomes ill during an important lesson), or may develop over a long period of time (as the result of the lack of recognition for continued successful achievement).

PERCEPTIONS AND IMAGES OF THE TEACHING PROFESSIONS

One of the first sources of stress experienced by many educators is the realization that their expectations about the field vary significantly from day-to-day reality. When expectation and reality differ greatly, potential for career disillusionment can increase.

A list of stressors compiled by several groups of teachers showed that primary sources of tension and anguish were not the result of the basic teaching/learning process. The primary stressors listed by the teachers were:

—Clerical work
—Interruptions that disrupt class
—Discipline problems with students
—Lack of equipment and materials
—Lack of teacher input in decision making
—Rigid curriculum
—Destruction of school property
—Conflicts with administrators
—Problems with parents

—Class size
—Lack of planning time
—Problems with other teachers
—Feelings of powerlessness
—Problems with racist and sexist attitudes and actions (Alschuler, 1980)

Any teacher, regardless of years of experience, who is exposed to one or more of the above stressors over an extended period of time, is likely to feel the anguish of disillusionment with the educational system.

Until recently, few college- and teacher-orientation programs addressed these concerns openly. Instead, unrealistic expectations of the ideal classroom, ideal learner, and ideal system were fostered, as well as other commonly held but inaccurate images of teachers and their profession. Some of these include:

—The teacher as an admired public servant
—Teaching as a relatively easy task
—Infinite personal reward inherent in working with young people
—Teaching as a field in which the hours are short and vacations are long
—Teaching as a profession for women
—Teaching as a secure profession
—Teaching as a field in which support systems are many and effective
—The teacher and parent as an educational team
—The teacher as a professional above reproach
—The teacher as a miracle worker, with answers to all problems and cures for all
    learning weaknesses

Herbert Greenberg, in his text, *Teaching with Feeling,* referred to the ''burden of the myth'' of what a teacher should be. The myth states that a teacher must:

—Remain calm at all times
—Assume a philosophy of moderation in all things
—Place all students' feelings above his or her own
—Love all students
—Remain consistent
—Be permissive
—Hide his or her true feelings
—Have no prejudices
—Have no favorites
—Know all of the answers
—Make learning take place without confusion and uncertainty
—Cope with life without stress, anxiety, or conflict
—Teach students to cope with life without stress, anxiety, or conflict
—Protect students from negative feelings and situations (Greenberg, 1969)

Once established, these images, perceptions, and myths may hinder an individual's successful development as an educator. Today, many colleges and universities are working to prevent this by helping preservice teachers to recognize the realities and weaknesses of the field and take steps to cope with them.

Community Role Expectation

The community has perceptions and expectations of its educational system that place additional strain on the professional educator. What the general public expects of its educational system and the teachers is often different from the reality of service provided. It too holds certain beliefs that are often unrealistic. For instance, because a large percentage of most local government budgets goes toward education, the public often assumes that the system is well funded and all fiscal needs are being met. The community often sees the educational system as an extension of the home, mandating that educators teach values and instill discipline. Other people insist that the educational system is not an extension of the home and should not deal with values and discipline. The public expects the educator to educate, regardless of the student's motivation and limitations. It is difficult, at best, for many parents to accept that their child is not a genius. They place the blame for low achievement almost solely on the teacher and educational system. The public also demands input into its educational system, often to the point of challenging the expertise of professional educators. The public promotes innovation in its educational system but shuns involving students in experimental programs. It expects individualized instruction and growth of students as unique individuals, yet, complains when achievement on standardized tests does not compare favorably to the scores of large numbers of student groups. Members of the community sometime expect teachers to be above reproach, scrutinizing moral behavior and personal lifestyle. Finally, the public perceives a hierarchy in education, placing the college professor well above the elementary school teacher.

There are many other views and expectations held by the public. How educators and administrators respond to them may either create or resolve many stresses and strains. Because of their naturally differing points of view, there will never be complete harmony between educators and parents. Teachers and administrators who understand this divergence and work to promote positive interaction from it will have a minimum of conflict. Those who fight it will experience a higher degree of stress.

> A teacher can be a parent, but a parent is not a teacher. A parent's role is very different from that of a teacher. Usually a parent's concept of a child is very different, also. This is only logical. You as a teacher see the child as a student, one of an entire class. Children in a group do not behave as they would by themselves ordinarily. The leader, the follower, the bully, the loudmouth, and the meek are all playing parts that relate to their peers. At home the child is one of a much smaller group, some of whom are not peers but of an older generation. This fact underlies much misunderstanding between parents and teachers (Maggs, 1980).

Peer Expectations

In any profession, stress may be caused by the expectations or demands placed on an individual by colleagues. For instance, a practitioner's peers may expect him or her to work more or to work fewer hours. Peers have the ability to dictate the prevailing attitude toward the job at hand or the system as a whole.

On the other hand, colleagues may also play a dynamic role in making work an enjoyable experience. Peer expectation may challenge a worker to reach out and tax his or her potential. It may establish an environment of mutual support.

In education, the peer group may vary. It may be as simple as two or three instructors in the same team or sharing classrooms on the same floor of a building. It may be all of the teachers of a single grade level or of a particular subject. Or, it may be all of the teachers in a particular school. Regardless of size, the peer group maintains certain expectations of its members. When these expectations conflict with the individual teacher's goals, expectations, or work style, conflict and anxiety may occur and stress is created.

System Expectations

Every system places expectations on its personnel. Such expectations may be in the form of well-established, written policies, procedures, and directives, or they may be implied through conversation, actions of others, and tradition. When the system's expectations are unrealistic or unreachable, anxiety is created. If the evaluation of practitioners is based on these expectations, stress will develop. A person's sense of self-worth may be challenged as he or she develops a chronic sense of "I'm not good enough" or "I'm not all I should be" (Woolfolk & Richardson, 1978).

In education, the system's expectations change rapidly to accommodate new philosophies, community expectations, fiscal constraints, and more. At times, the expectations of the educational system seem to conflict with themselves (for instance, the simultaneous demand for individualized instruction and standardization).

When the system's expectations are too rigid, such as a curriculum guide that allows no flexibility for the classroom instructor, frustration surfaces. When the system's demands conflict with the needs of students, teachers may rapidly succumb to stress as they are pulled between two demanding forces. When the expectations of the system are in direct conflict with those of the teacher, there is a failed marriage.

> Tying one's self-worth to performance standards leads to excessive concern about other people's opinions. It results in fearful, alert looking to the reactions of others for clues as to where one stands in life or how one measures up in their eyes. Such concern, of course, is a sure recipe for stress (Woolfolk & Richardson, 1978).

Additional Myths

Some myths create a negative framework for the educator, that is, a foundation on which poor habits may be developed and educational controversies may rapidly grow. They don't just create expectations that differ from reality, but rather instill attitudes and perceptions that weaken the individual's potential for development as an innovative, exciting teacher. They create stress.

There are many fables and myths within the field of education according to Rothman (1977). Some of the myths serve only to feed the misperceptions that result in poor teachers and failures of the education system. Few of the myths have basis in fact (Rothman, 1977).

Rothman offers the following myths:

Teaching Is a Mystique.   The teaching process is mysterious, awesome, complex, wonderful, difficult, heartrending, indefinable, impossible, and heartwarming.

It's Never the Teacher's Fault When Children Don't Learn.   The myth that it is not the teacher's fault when students don't learn indicts students and, simultaneously, serves to absolve educators of any culpability. It is based on the premise that some students can't learn and some won't learn. In any case, it is the student's problem when learning does not take place, not the teacher's.

Teachers Know Best.   The myth that teachers know best eliminates alternatives and puts most things in a right or wrong category. The right or correct way is the teacher's way. Students must do what they are told.

Students Must Never Be Wiser Than Their Psychiatrist or Teacher.   To keep students in their proper place, they are grouped by teachers and the educational system. They are continuously separated on the basis of achievement, intelligence, sex, and other factors. They are sometimes polarized and sometimes pitted against one another in their groups.

Learning Is Sequential.   The myth of sequential learning is based on the assumption that learning occurs in developmental, and therefore sequential, stages. It implies that educators ritualize learning by insisting that no student can acquire skills or concepts before having learned the preceding skill or concept. It eliminates the concepts of unpredictability and spontaneity.

All Teaching Must Be in English.   The myth that all teaching must be in English effectively eliminates the teaching of foreign language skills, as occurs in most other nations. It also stifles more than 5 million students who use other languages as their primary speech. It is an ostrich-in-the-sand approach.

Reading Is the Only Avenue to Learning.   The belief that reading is the only avenue to learning is based in history, when the educational system once offered very little in the way of instructional alternatives such as television and learning centers. Other avenues of learning have suffered as a result of the extreme emphasis placed on reading as the primary, and sometimes only, avenue to learning.

Reading Is a Book; Mathematics Is Numbers.   Instruction based on the myth that reading is a book and mathematics is numbers provides little or no contextual relationship between such subjects as math and music, psychology and literature, or language and science. Relationships, when they are recognized at all, are tangential. This is particularly true in high schools and in higher education where subject areas are delineated and content is maintained as pure.

Using "Have to" Is an Acceptable Technique. The phrase "you have to" is often used by educators and is deemed a powerful tool, a favorite stronghold. Teachers at every level imply that students *have to* learn. Students also *have to* show respect, be quiet, walk in line, learn to read, attend school, be polite, dress properly, and more (Rothman, 1977).

SUMMARY

Every person, upon entering a position, has certain expectations about that position. These expectations are based on personal views, myths about the field, and education received in preparation for the job. Similarly, almost all people place expectations on others and expect their peers to perform and react in a specific manner.

Every organization, regardless of its size, holds expectations of its employees. These may be stated concretely through written policies and procedures or may be implied through tradition and accepted practice. The community, too, has expectations of the people who serve it.

In education, myths, misconceptions, and conflicts abound. They lead individual practitioners, the community, and the educational system itself to hold expectations that may vary from the reality of day-to-day instruction. The result is increased anxiety, tension, and strain—*stress.*

The educator's expectations may be idealistic and may have been reinforced by his or her college instruction. The individual may adjust these expectations or may succumb early in his or her tenure to job stress. The teacher will also play an active role as part of a peer group that holds expectations of others.

The community's expectations of its teachers may vary from the educational system's expectations of its teachers or from the expectations of the teacher, personally. The community sees the educational system as a large entity within the governmental system that receives significant financial support and exists solely to serve. The community's expectations of its teachers are also fueled by the fact that its members are parents who have understandably biased views of their children that are often in conflict with those held by teachers. Community demands may, at times, seem unreasonable because of the varying points of view held by members. Yet, community input into the educational system is considerable.

The expectations held by the educational system may change according to new philosophies, fiscal contraints, and community expectations. When change occurs too frequently, opportunity for succumbing to stress increases. If the expectations of the system are too rigid, the teacher loses flexibility within the classroom and additional stress may be experienced.

In general, when there is a variance between expectation and reality, conflict may evolve. This may begin early in a teacher's career. Until the gap between expectation and reality is tightened, stress will continue to mount, causing educators to grow disillusioned with their system and the profession.

REFERENCES

Alschuler, A. S. *School discipline: A socially literate solution.* McGraw-Hill Book Co., 1980.

Greenberg, H. *Teaching with feeling.* New York: McMillan, 1969.

Maggs, N. M. *The classroom survival book.* New York: New Viewpoints Publishers, 1980.

Rothman, E. *Troubled teachers.* New York: David McKay Co., Inc., 1977.

Woolfolk, R. L., & Richardson, F. *Stress, sanity and survival.* New York: Monarch Publishers, 1978.

Chapter 3

The Role of the Teacher and Job Stress

How a teacher's role is defined and perceived may be either a cause of stress or a source of stress reduction. If the role is well defined, based on reasonable expectations, and clearly understood, the individual will generally feel comfortable in filling that role and meeting the demands of the school system. Employees in any field whose roles are well defined feel that they have an understanding of and control over the tasks to be accomplished. Conversely, when the role is ill defined or written in broad, general terms, the practitioner may feel discomfort and loss of control.

ROLE DEFINITION AND ROLE AMBIGUITY

When asked what obstacles prevented him from preparing a clearly defined role for the teachers in his system, one administrator commented that the number of variables to be considered increased almost daily. The bureaucracy had become too large, he added, to tie a teacher into a role that was defined in specific terms. Defining teacher competency as it relates to role definition was another obstacle cited. Biddle and Ellena (1964), for example, stated, ''The problem of teacher effectiveness is so complex that no one today knows what the competent teacher is.''

Just as a role defined in broad terms may reek havoc, so may one defined in terms so specific as to eliminate or stifle an educator's freedom in the classroom. Parents can freely choose their parenting style, and independently decide how they will teach their own children. However, teachers do not have the same alternatives. Their freedom of choice is limited by institutional or organizational factors. Teachers are members of a system of policies, procedures, prohibitions, and norms that strongly influence how they respond to and teach students. When teachers are ineffective in facilitating learning, to some extent their failures may be attributed to organizational factors that define and limit the role of the teacher (Gordon, 1974).

Defining the teacher's role is a complex, confusing, difficult chore. It may be influenced by superintendents, principals, teachers, and unions, all of whom want to achieve effectiveness in the classroom and a balance between total freedom and a restrictive environment.

External influences, such as parents, independent school boards, and politicians have an impact on role definition. For example, a Syracuse, New York, teacher noted that educators are being required to assume broader roles, yet they are frequently criticized by the public. Subjects once taught within the family unit and church, such as sex education and moral education, are now the responsibility of the classroom teacher. Teachers even administer breakfast programs. Parents who demand that schools return to the basics (reading and math) also demand that teachers provide their children with discipline and teach them right from wrong (Landsmann, 1978).

No Simple Answers

There are no simple answers to questions about the role of teachers, whether they be in an elementary school in a wealthy suburb, an inner-city high school, or an ivy-league college or university. In fact, there are more questions about the teacher's role than there are answers. Many of these questions address deep philosophical issues, some of which are at the foundation of the concerns that exist in today's educational system.

—Who should be involved in defining the teacher's role? Teachers? Administrators? Parents? Students?
—Should the focus of attention be placed on the return to basics (reading, writing, arithmetic)?
—How much influence should unions and teachers' organizations play in defining roles?
—Is teaching a science or an art?
—Should the teacher assume roles that were once the sole responsibility of parents and family?
—Is administration and management so straight-jacketed by regulations and financial restrictions that redefining the role of teachers is an impossibility?

These are a few of the questions that surface in considering the duties to be performed by the educator. There is little clear agreement among the experts in answering them.

An educational philosopher once said that if the system is to free students in the classroom, it must first free teachers. He recognized that teachers are not free. Like students, they are controlled and directed by power and authority. At times, their own rights are not honored. In some systems, they do not participate in decisions that they are expected to carry out or enforce. Administrators often lack empathy and understanding when listening to the concerns of educators. They constantly work in an atmosphere of evaluation, judgment, and, sometimes, fear (Gordon, 1974).

Management, too, is hindered in defining the teacher's role. Those who set policy and administer the schools have lost many of their prerogatives. Principals who are supposed to provide leadership in the school are rendered impotent by a myriad of regulations and contractual restrictions. They find it difficult to maneuver. The combination of judicial restraints and requirements of teachers' unions has eroded the ability of many principals to manage their personnel (Maeroff, 1982).

CONFLICTS IN UNDERSTANDING THE ROLE OF THE TEACHER

It is clear when reviewing job descriptions for teachers that the role of the teacher is not easily defined and that the variables that come into play are growing more complex. Some descriptions establish the teacher as the all-knowing, all-doing, all-seeing paragon of excellence. Other job descriptions establish the teacher as an educational generalist, while some specify him or her as a specialist. Some of the job descriptions cite the teacher's role of establishing values while others restrict the teaching of values. Some job descriptions define the teacher's role to include such terms as "equipment manager" and "facilities planner." Others use terms such as "audio-visual equipment coordinator" and "meetings facilitator."

However, few role or job descriptions cite the uneven nature of teaching. They fail to identify such activities as crisis intervention, use of discretionary thought on a moment's notice, involvement in two or more tasks simultaneously, or providing discipline to the undisciplined. The lack of a practically defined role—one that is understood and representative of the actual tasks to be performed—is a stressor. The remainder of this chapter describes some of the areas in which teachers experience distress because of the various roles they are expected to perform. Such roles are rarely defined in a job description or presented to teachers as expectations of their school system. These roles include performing activities such as assuming responsibility for the general well-being of others, working long, unusual hours, and participating in planning and evaluation processes.

ROLE OVERLOAD

Most educators experience role overload. Role overload is an irregular work pattern common to the human services professions. Daily routines in the classroom may be broken by sudden crisis or disruption. These may include crises caused by students, the administration of the individual school, or the system itself. Any teacher who has experienced a fire drill in the middle of an important lesson and the subsequent disruption it causes has dealt with role overload. An educator who has to attend to a student who has become ill and requires immediate attention has experienced it. So has the teacher who has spent long hours in the evening preparing lessons for the next day's class session.

Role overload may also include exposure to long periods of boredom or routine activities, common in some assignments. Like too much activity in a given period, long periods of tedium and repetition can tax a person mentally and physically. It also includes use of discretionary thought without clear guidelines, as in the case of an educator who must make a disciplinary decision. Will there be repercussion? Will the system support the teacher? How far may the teacher go in disciplining a student? What degree of accountability does the system apply to discretionary decision making? Does the system purposefully promote the educator's use of discretionary decision making because firm policies and procedures are nonexistent?

Polyphasic Thought

Another role that almost every teacher assumes is that of the polyphasic thinker. Polyphasic thought is simply the task of thinking of two or more things simultaneously. Teaching a lesson and monitoring classroom discipline at the same time clearly involves polyphasic thought.

The process of polyphasic thinking becomes commonplace for most educators. In fact, there is little time during the workday when educators' thought processes are not polyphasic. Thus, polyphasic thought is also very tiring, although few people recognize it as a cause of fatigue.

RESPONSIBILITY FOR OTHERS

Almost all teachers take their responsibility for the education of their students seriously. While some critics of today's educators counter this, there are few people who would remain in teaching if it were not for a sense of responsibility for the well-being of others.

> Teachers come into teaching dewey-eyed and full of ideals. Perhaps years ago, particularly during the depression years, teachers came into teaching less out of idealism and more out of need for financial security. This is not true today. Other professions pay equally well, if not better, and are equally secure. The young people who are attracted to teaching today are generally motivated by an intellectual conviction. They want to do good. They want to be good (Rothman, 1977).

Many of the success stories of the American educational system are due, in part, to the dedication of teachers and the responsibilities they willingly assume. While often overshadowed by media and public criticism and a myriad of administrative responsibilities, the dedication to students' well-being held by most teachers has remained strong over the years.

Inherent in assuming any responsibility is a certain degree of stress. For example, a person taking a loan for a new home, a parent considering the future of his or her child, and a college graduate starting a new job have all assumed responsibility that may cause stress. This stress may be positive. In most cases, it is the type of stress that leads a person to tax his or her potential and meet the demands presented.

In some cases, though, this sense of responsibility can be overwhelming. Conflict may evolve when administrative and other demands interfere with meeting responsibilities. Whether perceived or real, once an educator judges that the system is making it difficult or impossible to effectively teach students, negative stress may develop.

Because educators care about their students and have a genuine desire to serve others, they often take on more responsibilities than can be reasonably handled. This, too, may cause negative stress. Failure to recognize personal limitations, as demonstrated by taking on too many tasks too often, has led many people to suffer from illnesses and disorders associated with stress.

> People who choose to go into the relatively low-paying helping professions usually have a sense of mission. They are compassionate and caring, which makes them especially vulnerable to the excessive demands that are made on them. The population they're dealing with is in extreme need. It is composed of troubled or deprived human beings with a void so huge it is almost impossible to fill it. These people take, drain, demand. They require continual giving and assume an endless supply on the part of the helper. Unless the worker remains aware of his limitations as a human being, he will burn out. And once he does, the conditions of the job will speed him on his way. If, as is common, the rest of the staff is harried and busy, they can't be counted on to supply an occasional compliment or the kind of morale boosting that could help (Freudenberger, 1980).

Once an educator falls into a system of regularly assuming too much responsibility, a series of events takes place. He or she may find that every day is overplanned. When this occurs for too long a period, it becomes the norm. The individual begins living a life in which there is a constant sense of time urgency and seems trapped. Even if everything could be accomplished in a given day, he or she will impose other tasks on the schedule, once again falling into the "not enough time syndrome." Eventually, performance suffers as speed rather than a sense of purpose becomes the priority. The person feels driven and will work a 50- or 60-hour week most of the year.

While still wanting to achieve perfection, the individual becomes frustrated. The hectic lifestyle and myriad responsibilities preclude achieving a high level of quality in accomplishing tasks. This then causes additional frustration as he or she feels increasingly dissatisfied with achievements (Forbes, 1979). Eventually, the primary task of helping students to learn is overshadowed by the task of stretching time. In this situation, everyone involved—students, parents, the school system, and the educator—loses.

PARTICIPATION

One of the best tools available to an administrator for motivating employees is involving them in the planning and evaluation of tasks and activities. Employees who are involved in such processes are generally more content and function better as team workers. When educators contribute to the decision-making, planning, and evaluating processes, they, too, achieve a higher level of job contentment. Through soliciting their participation, administrators acknowledge the employees' expertise.

However, a balance must be maintained. When a teacher assumes too great a role in the planning and evaluative processes, the instructional program may suffer. Meetings may be too frequent. Research and report preparation may grow too time consuming. The primary role of the teacher may become secondary.

Conversely, when an educator does not participate at all in the planning and evaluative processes within a college, school, or system, he or she may surmise that the administration cares little about employees' input or has little faith in such input. In either case, stress develops.

The areas outside of the classroom in which educators may, and often do, play a role are many and include, among others:

—Curriculum development
—Fiscal planning
—Planning of extracurricular activities
—Planning of disciplinary systems
—Planning of student conduct codes
—Planning for use of resource agents and specialists
—Planning for use of instructional television and media
—Planning of inservice training programs
—Public relations coordination
—Internal newsletter development
—Planning coordination with parents
—Development of grading systems

The level of involvement teachers have in these activities varies significantly from school to school and system to system.

WORK SCHEDULE

Another aspect of the teacher's role that may cause considerable stress is the work schedule. There are still people who think that the educator's work schedule includes only the hours that school is in session. In fact, the schedule of an effective teacher may infringe on time for family and for social and recreational activities. Lesson plans must be developed, papers must be read and graded, report cards must be prepared, and activities must be coordinated. Even when a part of the standard workday is allocated for these functions, there is rarely enough time to complete them. As a result, many of them are carried into the home to be accomplished in the evening or on weekends.

In addition, many educators participate in the extracurricular activities of their students, most of which occur after the "normal" school day has ended. Some schools and colleges require faculty to participate in such activities. Others offer salary bonuses and other types of financial incentives to promote such participation.

Since the frequency of both parents working outside of the home is greater than ever before, teachers must wait until evening to hold phone conversations with parents. Specialists and resource agencies may also have to be contacted after the school day or class sessions have ended. Many meetings set up by the system or by professional organizations are held in the evening or after the end of the school day. If an educator wants to enroll in graduate courses, these, too, must be scheduled beyond the normal workday.

As a result, most educators work long days and, often, long evenings. This affects their families and friends and sometimes their own health. If allowed to continue on a regular basis for too long a period, stress develops.

SALARY

Salary is another factor that affects the role a teacher plays within a school. It can affect a person's attitude and morale within the school, his or her self-concept, and even relationships with family and friends. While a teacher is an educated, skilled professional, he or she rarely earns a salary equivalent to other professionals. Of course, anyone who enters the education profession with the preconceived notion of achieving wealth will inevitably be doomed to a stressful life. Teaching is not, nor will it ever be, among the highest paid occupations. However, many teachers feel stress as they argue for salaries that they judge equitable and fair for the work performed and preparation required.

Again, most teachers entered the field to serve students. They did not enter it to participate in collective bargaining meetings or strikes. Yet, long-term collective bargaining situations and even teacher strikes are on the increase. This situation causes stress for everyone involved in the educational system and often forces teachers to play a role that they did not anticipate.

Controversy over teachers' salaries is not new; however, the number of teachers and teachers' organizations playing an active, visible role in matters related to salary and benefit packages has increased dramatically in recent years. Topics such as the educational mandates required of teachers, their duties and responsibilities, and demands made on them have long been items discussed in salary negotiations. Comparisons between education and other professions have also been made during salary negotiations for many years. As one text noted in 1828:

> It has always been surprising to me, that people in general are more willing to pay their money for anything else, than for the one needful, that is, for the education of their children. Their tailor must be a workman, their carpenter, a workman, their hairdresser, a workman, their hostler, a workman; but the instructor of their children must work cheap! (Bingham, 1828).

There are no simple answers to the controversial questions surrounding salaries in the field of education. Should an elementary school teacher be paid more or less than the college professor? Is there a sound basis for paying higher wages to an educator who has obtained graduate credits, even though he or she is performing the same work as those with four-year degrees? Are there valid standards by which a teacher's remuneration may be judged? Can it be assumed that increased salaries will equate to a better quality of instruction in the classroom? The issue of increased pay for teachers is mired with questions and controversies.

> What should a teacher be paid? No salary is enough for a good teacher, for one whose contribution is not realized alone in skills learned but is evidenced in the ability of people to learn to live peacefully, govern justly, and work creatively. His [or her] influence is not measured in numbers or words correctly spelled. It is not limited by a classroom door or the ringing of a bell. A teacher's impact knows no intellectual, physical, or time boundaries. How much does society owe in pieces of eight to Michaelangelo, Pasteur, Jonas Salk, or Albert Schweitzer—or to their teachers? What should an inferior teacher be paid? Anything is perhaps too much! (Ohles, 1970).

SUMMARY

Various aspects of the educator's role have been discussed. These range from ambiguity in how the role is defined to the lack of understanding of the significance of the educational process and the impact this has had on teachers' salaries. A lack of a clearly defined role, in any organization, may be a primary source of stress to practitioners. Ambiguity and conflict about the role can take its toll in increased anxiety and decreased productivity. If, in filling a particular role, an individual also assumes responsibility for the security and well-being of others, additional stress may be realized (Yates, 1979).

Conflicts in understanding the role of today's educator abound. These conflicts often have their foundation in the myths and misconceptions that shroud the education profession. They also have their basis in the myriad demands made upon today's educators by the students they serve, the community, and the educational system itself.

Everyone seems to have a personal opinion about the educational process and how teachers should participate in it. Critics of the educational system include students, parents, school administrators, community leaders, union leaders, special interest groups, and the teachers themselves. As a result, explaining the role of the educator in precise, measurable terms remains difficult.

There are also conflicts inherent in the duties performed by most educators, making role definition difficult. Teaching is an uneven, imbalanced process. In one moment, a teacher may be responding to a crisis involving a student or the school system. In another, the teacher may be enduring long, tedious periods in the classroom, on cafeteria or bus duty, or in preparing report cards and other documents. Teachers must make discretionary decisions every day. While they are held strictly accountable for the consequences of these decisions, there are very few guidelines and very little instruction offered on how and when to use discretionary judgment.

Time is a major constraint interfering with a clearly defined role. Little time is allowed to perform all of the tasks that must be accomplished in order to effectively educate others. Throughout the workday, most educators are involved in a mental process known as polyphasic thought, thinking of two or more things simultaneously. Mental "down time" is almost nonexistent, even during so-called breaks. Despite this reality, the general public often perceives educators as having a great deal of time on their hands, with short work hours and summers off.

Most educators take the responsibility for the well-being of their students seriously. This is an asset that is often taken for granted. Anyone, regardless of his or her profession, who assumes responsibility for the care, guidance, and growth of others is bound to experience stress. When this responsibility is overshadowed by administrative, political, public relations, and fiscal concerns, the negative effect of stress is compounded.

A teacher's participation in the planning, decision-making, and evaluation processes of his or her educational system or school, or the lack of such participation, may also be a primary source of stress. What role should a teacher fill in participating in processes traditionally left to administrators and managers? If there is no participation, stress may be experienced. If there is too much, stress may also become excessive. The participative process is becoming better defined in many school systems and higher educational institutions, acknowledging the expertise of teachers. The participative role of teachers may be extended to such areas as curriculum development, planning of extracurricular activities, development of standards for students, public and parent relations, planning of inservice training, and more. When the participation process is open and strong, without being excessive, the negative effects of stress may be reduced.

Of all of the issues resulting from the lack of a clearly defined role for today's educator, none has received as much attention as salaries. Educators have unionized and have gone on strike. Through their professional associations and organizations, they have launched large-scale national public relations campaigns to get the public to understand their plight. While great wealth and high earnings will never be synonymous with the field of education and while most educators realize and accept this, there remains great controversy over the inequities between teacher salaries and those of people in other human service professions.

From state to local government, school system to school system, and teacher to teacher, the role of the modern educator is defined differently. While all may agree that the primary goal is to assist students to learn, few will agree on anything more precise. Myths and misconceptions abound. There are varying levels of community involvement in the educational process and varying fiscal constraints affecting duties and responsibilities of teachers. All of this results in a role for today's educator that is generally broad based and ill defined. This, in turn, results in increased anxiety and, perhaps, job disenchantment. The degree of job stress experienced may be directly related to the clarity of definition of the role teachers are required to fill.

REFERENCES

Biddle, B. J., & Ellena, W. J. *Contemporary research on teacher effectiveness.* New York: Holt, Rinehart and Winston, 1964.

Bingham, C. *The Columbia orator.* Boston: J. H. A. Frost, 1928, p. 165.

Forbes, R. *Life stress.* New York: Doubleday & Co., 1979.

Freudenberger, H. J. *Burnout: The high cost of achievement.* New York: Anchor Press, 1980.

Gordon, T. *T.E.T.—Teacher effectiveness training.* New York: Peter H. Hyden Publisher, 1974.

Kohl, H. *On teaching.* New York: Schocken Books, 1976.

Landsmann, L. Is teaching hazardous to your health? *Today's Education,* 1978, April/May.

Maeroff, G. *Don't blame the kids.* New York: McGraw-Hill Book Co., 1982.

Ohles, J. F. *Introduction to teaching.* New York: Random House, Inc., 1970.

Rothman, E. *Troubled teachers.* New York: David McKay Co., Inc., 1977.

Yates, J. *Managing stress.* New York: American Management Association, 1979.

Chapter 4

Stress and Daily Tasks

For most teachers, stress may come from several areas in their daily functioning. These include daily functioning on the job, interacting with supervisors and administrators, functioning in the home, and interacting with family. Stress may also be related to social life and self-image. Each area is significant in fostering or reducing stress.

There are many stressors inherent in both the routine and nonroutine tasks performed every day by an educator. Many educators learned to prepare themselves for dealing with these stressors and strains associated with their daily tasks because, previously, they were not mentally and emotionally preconditioned to cope with them. Some who cope well initially still find that they succumb to the stresses and strains after devoting many years to the profession.

USE OF AUTHORITY AND DECISION MAKING

The stresses and strains associated with the daily functions of educators are as many and varied as the tasks they perform. One area of functioning on the job that often creates stress is the area of authority and decision making. Most educators assume that they have certain authority to control their curriculum, manage their class, and determine the educational techniques to be used with individual students. However, fixed authority within the hierarchical structure of the school is often unclear. Many teachers simply assume authority to accomplish certain tasks.

> Being a teacher is being smack in the middle of the social system of the school. The students and nonprofessional adults are underneath, and the administrators and all the bureaucrats at the central district office, as well as the school board, are above. There is status to the role and a certain amount of power and independence within

one's own classroom. However, the teacher is subject to demands from below and directives from above. . . . However discontent most teachers might be with the social system as a whole, they obey certain rules in order to protect their status and maintain some solidarity as a group. . . (Kohl, 1976).

Curriculum Development Decisions

Nowhere is the educator's authority more important than in structuring subject curriculum to be presented. Stress arises in some school systems when the teacher is not given sufficient authority to make the decisions he or she is most qualified to make. Stress may also arise if too little guidance is provided in structuring the curriculum.

Classroom Management and Discipline Decisions

Stressful situations also erupt when classroom management and discipline decisions are questioned. Without doubt, teacher authority and classroom discipline are two of the areas of greatest controversy in modern education. Most people acknowledge that teachers must be able to discipline in order to maintain order and provide an adequate environment for instruction. But, the controversy centers on the meaning of discipline and how it should be used.

According to Ohles (1970), it is difficult to determine whether the primary purpose of some schools is controlling and disciplining students, or providing a worthwhile learning experience. It is clear that learning cannot occur in an environment in which either anarchy or turmoil exists. The ideal classroom environment is one in which enthusiastic, competent teachers and exciting, rewarding experiences establish an atmosphere suitable for learning. However, the disappointing reality is that there is an excessive dependence on the use of teacher authority to establish behavioral patterns suitable to classroom learning (Ohles, 1970). Too few teachers are prepared or willing to commit the time and energy required to establish the ideal classroom environment.

Classroom discipline, when not properly administered or when not supported by the school system, often evolves into the greatest of all forms of discouragement to the educator. After all, individuals join the profession to help students learn and not to function as disciplinarians.

> Apparently the majority of teachers begin their professional lives with the idea that they will experience feelings of joy and accomplishment, but instead find school life filled with strife, a world where they feel pitted against their students in what often seems to be a struggle for survival. When teachers experience this letdown, they try to figure out what happened. They know something went wrong and they feel there must be some explanation for why teaching isn't the satisfying job they anticipated it would be (Gordon, 1974).

Interacting with Parents

Teacher authority is also a source of question when it comes to interacting with parents. There are those administrators who strongly encourage interaction and provide authority to educators to do so as often as possible. There are others, however, who strongly discourage interaction between teachers and parents, holding it to the minimum required to meet the demands of the school system.

Generally, parents have not been provided the information they need to understand modern instructional techniques. As a result, they may readily question an instructor's approach or teaching style. They may doubt the value of the instructional program. A teacher who has been given the opportunity to orient parents and keep them informed through an open system of communication will maintain an effective relationship throughout the school year. Students, parents, and teachers benefit and stress is avoided or reduced.

Conversely, a teacher who is stifled in her or his attempts to interact with parents may face a term of criticism and question. The student, parents, and teacher suffer, as does the school system. Stress is increased.

Grading

Grading students may also be stressful. One of the most frequent criticisms of today's educational system focuses on the advancement of students who do not have basic skills. Some teachers readily complain that parental pressure on administrators may cause this. Others state that pressure to advance students against the recommendation of teachers comes directly from the system's administration that places greater emphasis on positive community relations than on effective instruction. Under such pressure, an educator will feel stifled, question his or her worth to the students and the system, and experience increased stress.

For many instructors, the grading system does not mesh with their own philosophies. Some do not believe in a system that "fails" or labels students. Stress evolves when the variance between personal philosophy and system mandates is great.

Making Referrals

Finally, stress is experienced when educators lack the decision-making authority to obtain support for students with special needs in order to provide them with the best education possible. When referral to an available specialist or resource agency cannot be made because of red tape, lack of authority, or lack of space in special classes, the teacher will become frustrated and angry. These emotions are manifested in increased stress.

HUMAN EMOTIONS AND DAILY TASKS

Every day, in the performance of daily tasks, educators experience, hold, share, and vent a variety of emotions. It is difficult—if not impossible—to work with a group of students for a lengthy period of time without experiencing emotion.

Students, particularly the young, express emotions readily, usually in a more free, open form than adults. Hate, joy, anger, sadness, fear, disgust, love, and other emotions may all be expressed in a single day or class session. The educator is expected to cope with this.

> Abilities, values, and prejudices are not isolated and unrelated factors. They are in large measure born and bred, controlled and expressed, maintained and altered, by means of emotions. The educative process is facilitated to the extent that the student accepts and understands his emotions and the teacher accepts and understands the emotions of the students and of himself. The impact of emotions in the classroom is eased by the general flexibility of a group of students and is further aided when a teacher is able to bend with the emotions of students (Ohles, 1970).

Venting Emotions

Stress may be related to emotions in a number of ways. A teacher who holds too many feelings within will soon find that they can erupt in the form of physical illness. He or she may vent them inappropriately at home or explosively at a co-worker or administrator. Emotions may also be released at students.

The "Ripple Effect" When such venting occurs, the educator develops feelings of guilt and embarrassment over having lost self-control. This creates additional stress. It may also have a rippling effect as the person toward whom the emotion was vented seeks retaliation in some form. For a student, this may be a complaint to a parent who in turn complains to the school's administrator. The incident may be cited in the teacher's evaluation as a weakness. In any case, stress is compounded when a teacher vents emotions explosively.

Sharing Emotions

It may also be difficult for a teacher to express emotions openly and calmly with someone in the educational system. Sharing emotions positively may occur in the home or social environment, but the spouse or friend may not have sufficient understanding of the educational process to provide support. Sharing with supervisors and administrators will occur only if they have established a positive framework for such interpersonal interaction. Sharing with peers will be contingent on the relationship that has evolved with them. If the relationship is positive, sharing emotions may occur. If it is neutral or negative, such sharing will be near impossible. The least stressful environment for the educator is one in which he or she may readily share emotions resulting from the teacher/learner/educational system relationship.

ACCOMPLISHING DAILY TASKS

So far, discussion has focused on those aspects of daily job functioning having to do with authority and emotions. Stress may also be experienced in the performance of basic classroom duties. Meeting student and school system needs is simultaneously a rewarding and difficult process.

Teaching, regardless of the subject area, is a complex process. It requires that the instructor and students work together toward a common goal. When obstacles arise in this endeavor, stress is experienced by both the learner and his or her teacher. If the teacher's daily tasks were limited to assisting students to learn, there would not be cause for as much concern as exists over job stress. But, the daily tasks of almost every teacher include a myriad of duties that go beyond functions associated with the teacher/learner relationship. In some schools and systems, these duties may require much more from the educator than actual in-class instruction and related preparation.

HOUSEKEEPING AND ACQUIRING SUPPLIES

At a casual luncheon meeting of several former teachers, one of the major criticisms of the educational process concerned the role teachers must play in performing general housekeeping chores and gathering the supplies and equipment necessary to perform their daily tasks. ''I was always begging and bartering for the supplies and materials I needed to teach my class. It was frustrating to begin every day wondering whether or not I'd have all of the books, papers, and audio-visual equipment I'd need to teach my lessons,'' one of them remarked.

Many educators spend a significant portion of their workday tending to housekeeping chores. To some degree, this is to be expected. In some school systems, however, the housekeeping chores performed by teachers are excessive. This may be due to a lack of personnel assistance or to a lack of resource materials. It may also be because others, such as secretaries and aides, are not required to perform more of the nonteaching duties usually accomplished by educators. In one elementary school, for example, there was one television to be shared by all of the classes. There was also a requirement that students participate in some of the state's instructional television programs. Each day, there was a ''battle'' among the faculty to determine who would have access to the equipment.

The use of paraprofessionals to perform some of the housekeeping chores traditionally performed by teachers has proven effective in many school systems. Research has shown that when these duties are left to paraprofessionals, the teacher is able to give better attention to students and make better use of time. In turn, job contentment is enhanced since the teacher spends more time helping others to learn (Maeroff, 1982). When housekeeping chores, such as arranging for facilities and equipment and cleaning up after such activities, grow too demanding, everyone suffers. The educator feels additional stress.

MEETINGS

One of the daily routines of educators that may cause stress is attendance at meetings. There are meetings for planning, evaluating, and sharing information, and for setting up other meetings. There are meetings with parents, students, supervisors, administrators, and peers. There are meetings when everything is going well. There are meetings when something goes wrong. And there are meetings to discuss the status quo. It seems as though there is an unwritten rule in many schools, colleges, and educational systems—when in doubt, hold a meeting.

Some meetings are important. They bring together groups of people to share information and approach issues collectively. Many meetings result in new or improved programs and techniques, new policies and procedures, and unity where there was once a divergence of opinions.

When meetings are conducted properly, everyone gains. But many meetings, regardless of their importance, present problems to those attending. Teachers regularly attend school-wide and system-wide meetings on a wide variety of topics including grade level or subject matter, curriculum, health insurance and other benefits, Christmas programs, scholarships, social activities, and American Education Week. Meetings are called by superintendents, deans, principals, and colleagues. They may also be called by parent-teacher associations, professional organizations, unions, business interests, and community groups.

Few meetings are well structured. The pattern of most teachers' meetings includes late starts, unrestrained parliamentary procedure, excessive argument, prolonged and unrelated discussions, personal frictions, politics, and delays of agenda items to future meetings. While some meetings in the field of education are efficient, effective, and rewarding, many are bungled and confusing (Ohles, 1970). They often create more strain and tension and cause more problems than they resolve.

TEACHING: HELPING OTHERS TO LEARN

The task of teaching others may be a source of stress even though it is the reason that most people enter the field of education. It is the task that provides the greatest reward when it is successfully accomplished. It is the process that tests the practitioner's skills and abilities and provides challenge.

Because there are so many concepts, techniques, issues, and details to consider when providing instruction to a class of students, teaching may cause mental strain or fatigue. That is not necessarily a symptom of negative stress but may be simply the tired feeling that follows a good day's work. Most teachers agree that it is impossible not to feel mentally, physically, and sometimes, emotionally drained after a successful day in the classroom.

In a single day of instruction, a teacher may have to give consideration to the following:

1. Ability of students to learn
2. Quality and availability of audio-visual materials
3. Behavior of students during the presentation of lessons

4. Motivation provided within the lesson
5. Individualization of instruction to provide maximum opportunity for each student
6. Established schedules for presentation of the curriculum
7. Homework and other assignments to be made and checked
8. Evaluation
9. Coordination of lessons with resource teachers and specialists

When these and other tasks associated with instructing become cumbersome or restrictive, negative stress may develop.

The basic task of helping others to learn is at the foundation of many current controversies in education. There are those who want educators to place greater emphasis on classroom instruction and the task of teaching. This group wants many of the extra tasks required of teachers to be eliminated. Others want teachers to continue and expand their daily tasks to include more out-of-the classroom duties.

SUMMARY

As with any profession, there are stressors inherent in the daily tasks performed by practitioners. In education, there are so many tasks to be performed every day that it is difficult to cite and explain them all. The daily duties performed by teachers also vary from system to system, school to school, department to department, and grade to grade.

When performing daily tasks becomes muddled with excessive red tape or questions of authority, the positive stress that is usually associated with a hard, full day's work may easily become negative. Frustration in accomplishing basic teaching tasks may be experienced.

Dealing with students is often stressful. Attending to the needs of a group of individuals in a confined environment for a lengthy period of time requires a great deal of stamina, dedication, and skill. In addition to contending with the individual needs of students in the classroom, educators must meet criteria established by administrators, curriculum committees, specialists, and others. They deal with the emotions, values, limitations, and strengths of their students every day. They experience the strain, anguish, and the rewards associated with this interaction.

Other daily tasks that are sometimes stressful to educators include: performing general housekeeping chores; attending meetings, conferences, workshops, and extracurricular programs; and teaching itself. In each of these areas, the potential for distress exists. The variables that make these chores either pleasant and rewarding or difficult and stressful are numerous. Administrative decisions, coordination and communication within the school, teacher preparation, and funding are but a few of the variables.

REFERENCES

Gordon, T. *T.E.T.—Teacher effectiveness training.* New York: Peter H. Hyden Publisher, 1974.

Kohl, H. *On teaching.* New York: Schocken Books, 1976.

Maeroff, G. *Don't blame the kids: The trouble with america's public schools.* New York: McGraw-Hill Book Co., 1982.

Ohles, J. F. *Introduction to teaching.* New York: Random House, Inc., 1970.

Chapter 5

The Educator's Job and Burnout

The average person spends a great deal of time on the job. If the workday is 8 hours, time on the job may represent one-half or more of the person's waking hours, 5 days each week. This does not take into account the time devoted to performing job-related tasks at home or the many hours people spend thinking about their work during their at-home or leisure time.

One of the first steps in controlling job stress is to understand the impact the job can have on a person. Such understanding helps a person identify those areas of the job that can be controlled or changed and those that cannot. People differ in the expectations they bring to their work. They differ in the satisfaction and rewards they derive from work. And, they differ in how they perceive their daily tasks, their supervisors, and their profession in general. If five teachers were asked to describe their reasons for entering the field and list the rewards they gain from it, it is unlikely that their answers would be the same.

Table 1 is an indicator of an educator's job-stress level. A person should check the statements in both column A and column B that apply to his or her feelings about the job.

Five or more checks in Column A suggest that a person is in a too-low stress zone. Five or more in Column B suggest too much stress. Four or more in each column suggest conflicting stress, which is also a performance problem. Those people who checked very few of the items may not be experiencing an appreciable degree of job stress. However, a person could check few items and still be highly stressed, depending in part on intrinsic interest in the job (Matteson & Ivancevich, 1982).

Table 1. Job-stress level

Column A

____ I have little variety in my job.
____ I am not challenged by my job.
____ I have too much time on my hands.
____ I wander around looking for things to do.
____ I have very little work to do.
____ I am simply bored by the routine of my job.
____ I have to push myself to stay alert.
____ I have too little responsibility.
____ I am overtrained for my job.

Column B

____ I have too much variety in my job.
____ My job is too challenging.
____ I don't have enough time to finish my work.
____ I don't have time to visit because of my workload.
____ I always have to take work home with me.
____ I am overwhelmed by the nonroutine pace of my job.
____ I never have time to recover from the pace of work.
____ I have too much responsibility.
____ I wish I had some training to do my job better.

FACTORS IN WORK AND STRESS

In their research, Appley and Trumbull (1967) identified those factors of a person's work that cause the greatest stress and strain. They conducted studies of both managers and workers to determine people's perceptions about their jobs and where they felt greatest change was needed. In some topic areas, their findings were surprising. They considered the following areas and asked both managers and workers questions about each.

Volume of Work Workload may be both a cause of stress and a stress reducer. Underwork can be more stressful than overwork. A large workload, if handled productively, can be restorative and can serve to reduce tension.

Impact of External Rewards on Successful Performance People work better when there is a good system of reward for successful performance. However, people also perform depending upon the magnitude of punishment or failure associated with unsuccessful performance. Where people are not held accountable for performing required tasks, levels of accomplishment will be low.

Ease or Difficulty of Work Ease or difficulty of work is not a critical determinant of job stress when compared to the consequences of success or failure. When a person can concentrate fully and become absorbed in a task, regardless of its difficulty, stress will be lower than if the person cannot give it full attention. In addition, tasks that challenge status, such as IQ tests or promotional exams, create stress regardless of their difficulty.

Existence of Deadlines People who know their job requirements, understand their own abilities and skills, and pace themselves efficiently are not as stressed by deadlines as those who do not. For all people, though, stress is related to the degree of punishment for failure to meet imposed deadlines.

Job Pressure Job stress is synonymous with strain, anxiety, tension, conflict, and pressure. It is a catch-all term that also parallels such terms as r ̮cdle, drive, sell, push, persuade, urge, coerce, and win. Job pressure is often related to management's philosophy toward employees. If managers see employees as hardworking, skilled individuals, job pressure will be less than if they view their workers as primarily lazy, unmotivated, undedicated, or unskilled. In studies, the primary job pressure was determining how to measure successful performance and productivity, a particularly difficult task in the field of education.

Benefits In studies, those workers and managers who felt the greatest degree of job stress also felt that their benefits were not very good. Workers with ample benefits felt less stressed toward their organization.

Communications Workers under stress felt that management did not listen to their ideas, they could not talk openly with people higher up in the administrative pyramid, and internal communication was generally poor. Workers and managers who were least alienated and felt least distress also felt that they were kept well informed by their organization.

Job Security Workers who felt that their agency was loyal to them and that there would always be a place for them felt the least amount of job stress. Those who did not have a strong sense of job security or felt uneasy about the economic health of their organization experienced the greatest amount of job stress.

Intrinsic Aspects of the Job One of the most significant findings of the studies of workers and managers was that those who felt the greatest amount of job stress did not get a feeling of accomplishment from their work, regardless of how much time and energy they put forth. Those who found intrinsic reward in the job itself experienced lower job-stress levels.

Opportunity for Advancement Both managers and workers who viewed their possibilities for promotion or formal recognition for performance as poor experienced high degrees of job pressure and strain. People who felt that they were "getting somewhere" and were able to progress to where they wanted to be experienced the lowest levels of job stress.

Management Regarding attitudes toward management, those people with the greatest job stress judged that they were simply numbers to management and that concern for the well-being of workers was not high on management's list of priorities. Conversely, those workers who judged that managers were genuinely supportive of their growth, progress, and well-being felt the least amount of job stress.

Attitude Toward Supervision   Workers under greatest stress judged that their supervision was poor, based on surveys of employee opinions. Workers under greatest pressure felt that there was a double standard in that their bosses were treated better than they were. Workers with low job stress judged that a strong, supportive relationship existed with supervisors.

Social Aspects of the Job   While social cohesion is no guarantee of low job-stress levels, employees who had a strong social relationship with other workers stated that they experienced fewer job pressures (Appley & Trumbull, 1967).

DETACHED CONCERN

Because so many aspects of a teacher's job may result in stress and burnout, steps must be taken to reduce stress. One of the first objectives educators should list in their stress-management plan is detached concern. This is a stress-control concept for people in all of the human service fields, developed to assist physicians in their medical practice. It is a stance in which a caring physician is sufficiently objective or detached from the patient to exercise sound medical judgment yet show enough concern to provide sensitive understanding and care. Detached concern is a balance that is hard to achieve and maintain.

Stress develops when an educator becomes so overly involved with his or her students or faculty that objectivity is lost and, therefore, the ability to serve others well is weakened. Complete detachment is equally, if not more, dangerous. Complete detachment, a loss of enthusiastic concern for students and the development of dehumanizing attitudes, is one characteristic of job burnout. Where there is excessive detachment, there is insufficient motivation to provide services successfully.

The concept of detached concern is a goal in the stress-management plan because it can make the difference between job satisfaction and job burnout for an educator. Achieving detached concern may involve establishing new or fresh attitudes, withdrawing from situations when warranted, or seeking guidance from peers and supervisors. The key to success is keeping the job in its proper perspective . . . an important, worthwhile, and challenging job. The specific stress reducers and controllers outlined in the remaining chapters of this text provide assistance in achieving this goal. By reaching this goal, job burnout in education, and the stress associated with it, will be avoided.

JOB BURNOUT

Job burnout has been informally defined as a state of mind that frequently afflicts individuals who work with other people (especially but not exclusively in the helping professions) and who pour in much more than they get back from the people they serve. The symptoms of job burnout are similar to the symptoms of stress detailed in the following chapters. Burnout among educators is accompanied by an array of symptoms that include a general malaise; emotional, physical, and mental fatigue; feelings of helplessness and hopelessness; and a lack of enthusiasm about work and perhaps life in general. Like stress, burnout attacks an educator silently and subtly over a period of time. Rather than resulting from one or two traumatic events, burnout sneaks up on the educator and is recognized only when there is a general erosion of the spirit.

It is ironic that the people who suffer from burnout most frequently, such as educators, physicians, social workers, police officers, and other human service workers, are the ones who initially seemed the least likely to suffer from the stresses and strains of their jobs. They approached their jobs with enthusiasm and caring, sensitivity, and willingness to serve others. They sought internal rewards and recognized that the tangibles, such as high salary and short work hours, would be nonexistent. Yet, for someone to burn out, he or she must first have been "on fire" about his or her work, highly motivated and idealistic. The result is that the very best people in the profession and the ones who have the potential to be the very best are the ones most likely to suffer job burnout.

In an interview, a former high school teacher stated:

I can't believe there was anyone more excited about getting into the classroom than I was. It was all I ever wanted to do. Then, I wasn't in the classroom very long before I began to feel it. The more I gave, the more it seemed that the school and the students took. By my fourth year, I knew I wanted out. I was feeling tired by mid-morning. My family could see the effects. My career was going downhill and I couldn't stop it.

The sentiments expressed by this former teacher echo the comments of many other current and former educators.

Burnout is a syndrome in which teachers experience emotional exhaustion and a reduced sense of personal accomplishment. This occurs even though there may be no reduction or weakness in their productivity. Burnout is a response to the chronic emotional strain that is inherent in dealing with the problems, growth, well-being, and care of others. It is considered one of the many responses a teacher may have to stress.

While burnout is a response to the stress that comes from the interaction between helper and recipient, it also causes additional stress (Maslach, 1982). This occurs when the teacher realizes that he or she is suffering burnout. Frustration then sets in as the teacher fights to overcome his or her feelings of emotional exhaustion. It becomes a vicious cycle.

Repeated emotional strain and the subsequent emotional exhaustion it causes form the foundation for burnout. An educator easily becomes emotionally involved in the accomplishment of tasks and with the well-being of his or her students. Most educators actually overextend themselves and then grow to feel that other people are making too many demands on them. They begin to feel drained and tired, physically, mentally, and emotionally. They find that their emotional resources are becoming depleted and sources of replenishment are lacking (Maslach, 1982).

People who suffer from job burnout have not necessarily given in to their distress. Most want to continue to give of themselves. They simply recognize that their internal motivators are gone or nearly gone. Often, these educators will cut back on how much they give to others, accomplishing only the bare minimum necessary to get the job done. Their hope is that the fountain of internal motivation will be magically replenished and again begin to flow freely.

A teacher commented to the author of an article on job stress:

> The more I taught, the more I sensed a common theme in all those requests for bathroom passes, pencil-sharpening permission and notebook paper: "Gimme some attention." The negative attention syndrome must be the curse of the teaching profession. Time and again, I encountered students who obviously had brought their hunger for attention (and their anger) to school. The scuffled in class, rapped books on desks, slammed cabinet drawers and threw punches across the aisles, to name some of the milder behaviors. Teachers are caught: they don't want to feed the negative behavior with screams and threats but can't teach effectively with the disruptions, either. As one elementary school coach told me, "They'll get you if you don't get them first" (Maslach, 1982).

In this example, where did the burnout begin? Did it begin when the teacher was assigned one too many disciplinary problems? Did it begin when the resource agents that the teacher called upon for assistance were unable to help? Did it begin when parents complained because they did not agree with the teacher's style? Or, did it begin during the preparation of the teacher in college when classroom management and proper techniques for classroom discipline were not addressed? Whatever its start, once burnout sets in, the effects are the same. Educators feel helpless and somewhat out of control. There is a tendency to feel trapped. Even when the educator makes the decision to leave the school room or the educational system, she or he may lack the energy, stamina, enthusiasm, and self-confidence necessary to find other work.

In "Blaming the Victim," Ryan (1971) summarized burnout in the field of education in poetry:

> I used to care,
> But I don't care much any more.
> I used to care
> That children had to sit still and be quiet
> And read pages 9 to 17
> And answer the odd numbered questions at the end of the chapter;
> But I don't care much anymore.
>
> I used to care
> That finishing the assignment is more important than learning the skill,

And getting the right answer is more important than understanding,
And apologizing is more important than being penitent;
But I don't care anymore.

I used to wake up in the night
And think about ways to teach children
To set goals and work toward them,
To make decisions and live with the results,
To work together.
But there were those who felt threatened
And those who felt frightened
Because my classroom was different.
Parents did not understand.
They listened to the evil insinuations and the confidential criticisms.
Their protests overwhelmed my sand-based supports.
I used to care,
But I don't care much any more.

Now I say
Sit down
Be quiet
Read pages 9 to 17
No exciting ideas disturb my sleep.
I haven't had a complaint in over a year.
Nobody seems to care
That I don't care much anymore.

One of the primary feelings that educators get when suffering from burnout is self-doubt. It appears to them that they are among a small few who are experiencing the frustrations and tension, helplessness, and loss of enthusiasm to such a degree that they ask themselves, "What is wrong with me? Why can't I be more like them?" This tends to cause them to mask their feelings by internalizing them. They may even work harder to cover up their feelings of self-doubt, thereby appearing more enthusiastic and harder working than usual. Some who internalize their feelings may become sarcastic or cynical, aiming their cynicism at the education system and others who they judge not to be suffering the same feelings. In reality, their feelings are shared by many others. But, because they are masked, their stress level mounts as they feel increasingly alone in their feelings of burnout.

IDENTIFYING ADDITIONAL CAUSES OF TENSION ON THE JOB

Being aware of causes of tension on the job is the first key to controlling and reducing stress. In previous chapters, causes of job stress have been detailed. The following list provides further insight into the causes of job-related tension. The list, developed by Dr. Martin Shaffer, a clinical psychologist and co-director of Stress Management Consultants, can help a person identify alternatives to eliminate tension on the job.

1. Noisy environment
2. Inadequate lighting
3. Poor ventilation
4. People working too close to each other
5. Stagnant positions (e.g., sitting or standing in one place for too long)
6. Doing what you have to do rather than what you want to do
7. Time pressures
8. Pressures (internal or external) for exceptional performance
9. Constant pressure to make important and high-risk decisions
10. Lengthy time between vacations
11. Frequent demands for overtime (and hence less leisure time)
12. Working with clients who have many personal problems
13. Working with people who are always serious
14. Doing work that involves mostly fine motor coordination
15. Doing tasks that require a lot of close visual work
16. Working with tense people or people who are always in a rush
17. Inadequate sleep
18. Inadequate diet
19. Cigarette smoking
20. Too much drinking of alcoholic beverages
21. Lack of exercise to relieve tension
22. Marital conflict
23. Psychological conflicts
24. Economic insecurity
25. Continuing low self-esteem (e.g., persistently recalling personal faults and weaknesses)
26. Major life changes
27. Unexpressed feelings
28. Lack of recognition for performance on the job (Shaffer, 1982)

Any one of these items may cause feelings of tension or strain. If they are frequent and/or persistent, they may be the primary cause of job burnout. An educator should identify which of the items causes the greatest stress and then seek alternatives (such as those offered in the following chapters) to avoid or reduce them.

SUMMARY

A person's job has a significant impact on his or her well-being. If all is going well on the job, it may enhance the quality of an educator's life. If the job causes strain and tension, the quality of life will be lessened.

Job burnout is a state of mind that afflicts individuals in the helping professions who give of themselves without reaping appropriate personal reward. The symptoms of burnout among educators include a general malaise, feelings of helplessness, mental fatigue, emotional fatigue, physical fatigue, and a lack of enthusiasm about their work. Burnout may result from prolonged job stress. Burnout may also be a cause of stress as the caring educator feels frustrated over his or her feelings of job dissatisfaction.

One of the first steps toward reducing job stress and burnout is understanding the impact the profession has on the individual. This chapter outlined aspects of an educator's job that should be considered in assessing causes of job stress. They include:

1. Volume of work
2. Impact of external rewards on successful performance
3. Ease or difficulty of work
4. Existence of deadlines
5. Unsatisfactory benefit package
6. Internal communications
7. Job security
8. Intrinsic aspects of the job
9. Opportunities for advancement
10. Management's concern
11. Attitude toward supervision
12. Poor or inadequate physical environment
13. Pressure to perform, meet deadlines, and make decisions
14. Time
15. Serving too many clients with varied personal problems
16. Physical habits such as eating, smoking, and sleeping
17. Personal or marital conflicts
18. Major life changes
19. Low self-esteem
20. Unexpressed feelings

This list represents a sample of the causes of job burnout. Once identified, the causes provide a foundation for the cure, that is, an educator will know what areas need to be addressed first in establishing a stress-management plan. Every educator should include detached concern as an objective in her or his stress-management plan. Detached concern is an attitude toward work in which the educator is sufficiently objective or detached from students, co-workers, and the internal workings of the system to make sound judgments, yet is able to show enough concern to provide sensitive understanding and care. Detached concern is a balance that is hard to achieve and maintain.

Later chapters in this book are devoted to various coping techniques. They offer suggestions for coping with and reducing stress. Programs, activities, and philosophies are offered that enable a person to establish and implement a stress-management plan.

REFERENCES

Appley, M., & Trumbull, R. *Psychological stress*. New York: Appleton-Century-Crofts, 1967.

Maslach, C. *Burnout: The cost of caring*. Englewood Cliffs, N.J.: Prentice-Hall, 1982.

Matteson, & Ivancevich. *Managing job stress and health: The intelligent person's guide*. New York: Free Press, 1982.

Ryan, K. *Teacher education*. Chicago: University of Chicago Press, 1971.

Shaffer, M. *Life after stress*. New York: Plenum Publishing Corp., 1982.

Chapter 6

Stress and Administration

Administration and management are vital functions in all professions. The physician who is self-employed must spend part of his or her time conducting business-related activities. The police supervisor must tend to such matters as scheduling, requisitioning supplies, and evaluating. The classroom teacher and college professor are also involved in day-to-day administrative matters.

Almost all employees interact with others administratively. They are either administered to by other people or they are required to direct people, things, or activities. Interaction in administrative matters is vital for effective and efficient functioning within an organization or agency. However, when the administrative process becomes burdensome or interferes with the accomplishment of tasks, stress results. In interviews with educators, many stated that the administrative or managerial-related stress that they experience causes them more problems and concern than any other form of strain or tension.

In previous chapters, many areas of stress directly related to the administration of the educational system were presented. Some of these areas were role definition, lack of recognition, and assignment to too many meetings. These represent only a few of the administration-related stressors plaguing educators.

ADMINISTRATION AS A MAJOR SOURCE OF STRESS

Stress resulting from the administration of an agency is common in bureaucracies. German scholar Max Weber originally defined the ideal bureaucracy as a social institution of professional people organized in a hierarchy and applying uniform standards to the handling of individual cases. Based on this definition, educational systems and institutions clearly aim to become effective, efficient bureaucracies.

By nature of their size and complexity, many bureaucratic organizations are slow and unresponsive. In the opinion of many, they resolve problems that began several years ago. At times, they appear more self-serving than public-serving in their nature and productivity.

Working in a bureaucratic organization can be frustrating for the best and most enthusiastic of workers. Ambitious, caring people want to see change and problems addressed rapidly. They want efficiency in service to their clients. They care and want to perform but, in many cases, the bureaucracy does not support them.

Educational institutions, whether they be large public school systems, private secondary schools, small colleges, or major universities, are among today's leading bureaucracies. Large budgets, complex systems of public accountability, independent boards interacting with public officials, attempts to meet the needs of growing user populations, and more, have, over the years, led to their current bureaucratic status. Everyone employed by the system or institution participates in the bureaucracy. Every employee performs certain tasks directly related to the bureaucratic system. For almost every educator, there are secondary duties, unrelated to his or her primary task, that must be accomplished because of the bureaucratic system than has evolved.

Responses to Bureaucracies

Veninga and Spradley (1981), through extensive research, found that people cope with these secondary, bureaucratic functions in five ways. They call these coping styles the loyal servant, the angry prisoner, the stress fugitive, the job reformer, and the stress manager. Educators may fall into one or more of the styles.

Loyal Servants Loyal servants are people who deal with their jobs by passive compliance. They simply follow orders and do the tasks assigned them. They may see themselves as hired hands who perform the basic duties required. They perform "by the book." They sometimes view people who are seeking change within the school or system as "troublemakers."

Angry Prisoners Angry prisoners are those who approach their job with passive resistance. Their job is like a prison, with no chance for escape or change.

> A teacher in an urban school described this feeling: "It's like I'm serving time in this school. My classroom has become a cell and I'm scared stiff to walk up and down the halls." Those who adopt a prisoner stance toward their jobs think they have no power to control their jobs. This same teacher said, "The parents have their ideas and control the school board; the administration's afraid to do anything; and the students have all the rights and freedom" (Veninga & Spradley, 1981).

Stress Fugitives Stress fugitives are people who turn and run from potential stress on the job. They go out of their way to avoid stressful tasks, procrastinate, and possibly neglect certain responsibilities. They prefer running to another task, transferring, or even resigning, to facing stressful tasks.

Job Reformers   Job reformers focus their coping energy on crusading for change. They often blame work conditions and the school system for all of the ills of the job. They dedicate themselves to coming up with ideas for change and then crusade to have the change implemented. They seek others to join their effort to initiate change or join other people whose ideas appeal to them. Resistance only causes them to fight harder or come up with new ideas for change.

Stress Managers   Stress managers attempt to identify and control job stress. They either employ personal strategies for coping or seek organizational strategies to effectively change a situation thereby making it as comfortable as possible. They work toward an honest understanding of their tasks, their agency, and their own attitudes toward the job. Examples of people who work toward managing their stress successfully are nurses who cry when a patient dies, salespeople who show their discouragement at declining sales, teachers who express their dismay when the system fails to respond to the needs of a student, and executives who openly discuss new career goals when they reach a plateau within their organization. They are not immune to the negative feelings associated with stress. They do, however, deal with these feelings openly and honestly. They do not pretend to be supermen and superwomen all of the time (Veninga & Spradley, 1981).

The five coping techniques cited provide an overview of responses to bureaucracies. Most people float from one type of response to another. Some people exhibit more than one response technique during a given workday, depending upon the nature of the stress at hand.

ADMINISTRATIVE STRESSORS

As stated, administrative stressors in education are numerous, as they are in many human service fields. Lourn Phelps of the University of Nevada identified 58 administrative stressors within the criminal justice fields. The findings are applicable to most human service professions and include such stressors as lack of recognition for achievement, poor relations with supervisors, excessive paperwork, lack of inservice training, lack of job security, and lack of promotional opportunity (Phelps, 1977).

Much of the stress in education is blamed on administrators and administrative functions. Some of these may be rooted in an individual administrator's work style. Quite often, though, administrators are blamed for processes and procedures that are not totally within their control to change.

Some of the categories in which stress is experienced by educators are:

—Policies and procedures
—Work schedules

—Relationship with supervisors, principals, and administrators

—Inconsistency among supervisors, principals, and peers
—Accountability for decisions made under pressure
—Response to complaints by parents
—Evaluation systems and measures of effectiveness
—Organizational rumors
—Physical resources
—Standardized tests as measures of student achievement
—Dress codes
—Work overload
—Budget and lack of fiscal support
—Public scrutiny
—Collective bargaining
—Teacher strikes
—Change
—Communication

A brief explanation of each of these categories of stress is provided in the following sections.

Policies and Procedures

In order for teachers to accept and implement policies and procedures of a school or entire school system, they should participate in the development of those policies and procedures. They are the ones who eventually must implement them. They are the ones who must interpret them and make them apply to the teaching/learning environment of the classroom. When teachers find policies and procedures unacceptable or so complex as to not be understood, they will either be hesitant in implementing them or will find ways to circumvent them completely. On the other hand, policies and procedures that reflect input by teachers are more likely to be implemented positively and in good faith (Anderson & VanDyke, 1972).

Work Schedules

Many educators work long days, arriving early and staying late. Many are required to attend evening meetings or feel the need to do so in order to be fully involved in their school's activities. In addition, many educators work long hours at home planning lessons, grading papers, and holding telephone conferences. When administrators or supervisors place pressure on the teacher to do so, either directly or through implication, strain and tension evolves.

Relationships

Good relationships with principals, administrators, and peers are vital to true job contentment. When the work environment encourages positive interaction among these people, everyone, including students, benefits. When poor relations exist among co-workers and supervisory personnel, finding job satisfaction will be difficult.

Inconsistencies

Conflicts and inconsistencies are inevitable in educational institutions where individuals are allowed to broadly interpret policies, procedures, and basic objectives (Levinson, 1970). When the priorities of supervisors and administrators are not consistent, teachers are unable to perform effectively. It is difficult to function efficiently in an environment where the teacher must jump from one task to another in order to please supervisors who failed to communicate with each other about the objectives to be accomplished. Where inconsistencies exist, conflicts are likely to occur. Severe stress will result and productivity will ultimately be reduced.

Accountability

Teachers and administrators are regularly required to make decisions. How top management personnel view this decision making has a significant impact on the level of responsibility an employee is willing to assume. When the system discourages educators from making decisions that are required for their effective performance, productivity will decline. On the other hand, teacher involvement and productivity is heightened when expectations for effective decision making are made known and such action is encouraged and supported. A proper balance must be maintained so that the authority of educators to make decisions is reasonable and consistent with the practitioner's skill level.

Response to Complaints

Employees in every field need to feel supported by the system that employs them. This support is vital to educators when complaints from parents or students are received. Such complaints are commonplace, as parents disagree with a program of learning or a grade given to their child. If teachers believe that the system does not judge them fairly or does not support them when complaints from parents or students are received, tension and paranoia will develop. Stress will result as teachers avoid making decisions or initiating action in order to avoid possible complaints.

Evaluation Systems

Generally, evaluation systems are one of the most controversial issues in personnel interaction (Wilson, 1977). Evaluation systems in education are used for a wide variety of purposes including measuring performance and serving as guides in determining promotions, transfers, salary increases, and disciplinary action. In some cases, using a single evaluation system or device to accomplish too many purposes weakens its effectiveness.

In many school systems, evaluations are conducted only once or twice a year. If these evaluations are used to make decisions about promotions and salary increases based on merit, employee disenchantment may result. The system measures only one or two class periods in the school year and may not reflect the employee's overall standard of performance.

The greatest stress evolving from evaluations in education occurs when the system being used does not adequately distinguish good, effective teachers from ineffective ones. For example, in one elementary school, all teachers were informed of the day that they were going to be evaluated in the classroom by the supervisor approximately one week before the evaluation would take place. For the good, effective teachers in the school, this was not significant. For one ineffective teacher, this provided sufficient warning so that he could prepare a sound lesson, borrow learning materials from other teachers, and rehearse his performance. When the evaluation took place, he received praise for his performance. Ultimately, he received the same salary increase and opportunities as his peers.

In education, as in any other field, recognition of achievement is necessary for job satisfaction. A weak evaluation system takes its toll in the form of excessive use of sick leave, job disenchantment, failure to openly accept new policies and procedures, and stress.

Organizational Rumors

A great deal of job stress in any field occurs if employees rely heavily on organizational rumors for information about administrative decisions, new programs, and other changes. When an effective system of communication between administrators and faculty does not exist, organizational rumors will be frequent. Rumors, particularly as they relate to personnel and administrative matters, cause stress because they are accepted as truth and create uncertainty.

Rumor Mill The best means to prevent the harmful effects of the rumor mill in any organization is through effective, widespread dissemination of facts before rumors can be started. There is no substitute for open, honest communication within an organization. A system of written directives and a carefully developed procedure of channeling communications up and down the chain of authority will reduce vulnerability to harm from the rumor mill. Regular information bulletins or newsletters will also serve to prevent and counteract rumors (Wilson, 1977). It should be noted, however, that no organization will be completely void of rumor. But, many of the problems resulting from the spreading of harmful rumors can be reduced or eliminated with some positive efforts toward more effective school-wide and system-wide communication.

Physical Resources

In education, one stressor almost always attributed to administration and management is inadequate physical resources to perform required tasks. Whether it be a lack of textbooks, a room that is too small, a heating system that does not work, or no place to relax between classes, anxiety and tension are created. Even the best employees experience job dissatisfaction if resources to accomplish tasks are inadequate for an extended period of time.

Standardized Tests

The debate over the value of standardized tests continues in education and among governing and political organizations. If a class, school, or entire system performs poorly on standardized tests, it is perceived to be less effective than a class, school, or system that scores well. Many variables, of course, influence these scores.

Standardized tests may provide some insight into student performance. The administration and faculty can learn about their educational programs. However, when the educational program revolves around getting students to score highly on standardized tests, stress evolves. The teacher may feel stifled in offering lessons that do not promote high student scoring on the tests.

When standardized test scores are not as high as some would like, the implication is that teachers are not performing successfully. Even other educators, such as college professors, criticize the failure of students to perform well in such subject areas as reading and grammar. They say student achievement is declining in general. In studies of various locales, such as one conducted in Edmonton, basic skills were shown to be the same or slightly higher among students studied over the period 1956–1977 (Truch, 1980), disproving allegations about student preparedness.

The issue of standardized tests is a controversial one. Some educators challenge the worth of standardized tests because they do not measure creativity and independence in learning. The controversy continues.

Dress Codes

Dress codes are a source of stress attributed to administration by many educators. In many school systems, dress codes for faculty do not exist. In some schools, the dress code for staff members is implied rather than written.

According to some administrators, there is as much merit for dress codes for educators as there is for people in business and industry. A faculty member dressed in jeans and a T-shirt will convey a certain image to students, parents, and others. Just as dress may not influence the quality of instruction, it also may not convey the image desired by administrators who must consider the public being served and community perception. Some people feel, too, that the standards established by educators serve as models for students. In any case, if a dress code exists in a school or system, the reasons for its existence must be well conveyed to all employees. When given sound reasons, most educators will respond favorably to the policy. When communication about the code is poor, the policy will be open to interpretation by individuals. Tension and anxiety may result.

Work Overload

When workers are given too much to accomplish in a period of time, stress occurs. Workload may be dictated by written directive or may be implied. Implied workload includes such things as expecting teachers to prepare grade reports or learning centers at home on their own time, or subtly requiring attendance at after-hours meetings.

Every employee needs a balance between work and leisure. When the school system interferes with this balance by dictating an excessive workload, stress will be experienced.

Budget and Fiscal Support

When asked why his faculty had no input into the school's budget, an administrator said, "The teachers don't have a real interest in fiscal matters. They're only concerned about what goes on in their classroom." The question arises whether the administrator can plan a budget effectively if he or she does not solicit input from faculty about what is going on in the classroom.

Most educators are aware of and concerned about the impact of budgeting on their job. Most, too, welcome the opportunity to be involved in the process that determines the degree of fiscal support provided to new and ongoing educational programs. This is particularly true in a period of increased fiscal constraint. An educator who sees budgets tightened, programs cut, and staff laid off experiences stress. Involvement in and understanding of the fiscal processes of the institution or school system aid in alleviating some of this stress.

Public Scrutiny

Along with other governmental bodies, the educational system has come under greater public scrutiny in recent years than at any other time since World War II. Politicians, special-interest groups, citizens, and educational organizations are checking and rechecking to ensure that the educational system is meeting their needs. As already stated, there are increased fiscal constraints being placed on the educational system and, with these comes additional scrutiny to ensure maximum efficiency for the dollars provided. Most educators have heard criticism of their system at social functions or read about them in editorials. Stress is inherent in such scrutiny. When educators do not feel protected against undue scrutiny, stress will be compounded and attributed to administration.

Collective Bargaining

Collective bargaining has been seen as both a friend and foe of education. Regardless of opinion, the stressors related to collective bargaining are numerous. For administrators, supervisors, and teachers involved in the bargaining process, there are many stressful and challenging hours spent in meeting each other's needs. For employees who must wait to learn the final outcome of the bargaining process, stress mounts.

There is little doubt that many benefits have resulted through the collective bargaining process. Many attribute much of the growth of the educational system and its employees in the United States to collective bargaining. However, most acknowledge that the collective bargaining process makes adversaries of members of the system, at least for a brief period during negotiations.

Teacher Strikes

At the beginning of every school year, national news programs and major newspapers and magazines headline teacher strikes in major cities and small towns.

The right of teachers to strike has been debated for many years. Some people feel that they have as much right to strike as any other workers. Others judge that teachers fall into the same category as firefighters and police officers and should be prohibited from striking.

For teachers who strike, those who do not, administrators and supervisors who cannot, and parents and students, a strike is stressful. The longer the strike, the greater the strain. Clearly, it is one of the most difficult, tense, and stressful situations in education.

Change

Change can be a significant stressor, and administration often takes the blame for such stress when change is frequent and/or unexplained. Girdano and Everly (1979) point out that the twentieth century is the "era of change." Recently, change in education has been frequent.

Most people have been reared to accept change and recognize that it is often good and desirable, leading to an easier or more productive life. However, Alvin Toffler, in his book *Future Shock,* noted that although change is a necessary part of society's behavior, it ceases yielding rewards if it occurs too frequently or too intensely. In this case, change can be devastating.

Toffler goes on to state, "We are simultaneously experiencing a youth revolution, a racial revolution, a sexual revolution, a colonial revolution, an economic revolution, and the most rapid and deep-going technological revolution in history" (Toffler, 1970). Missing from Toffler's list is the education revolution. There is little evidence to show that the rate of change in the field of education will cease in the near future.

When change becomes excessive or occurs without explanation or reason, stress evolves. A classroom teacher who is required to change the way in which grades are reported term after term will grow frustrated unless given sound reasons for the change. The supervisor who is told that the evaluation system for faculty is being changed without explanation may grow disenchanted if other changes of this type have occurred over a short period of time. While most educators recognize that the field is dynamic and changing, excessive, unexplained change may lead to job discontentment. Such change almost always will be blamed on the administration.

The importance of change as a stressor associated with administration and management cannot be understated. The Holmes and Rahe Social Readjustment Scale (see Chapter 8 for an in-depth discussion), a widely accepted measure of stress, is based primarily on life changes, both positive and negative. When change occurs in a person's professional, family, and social life, coping may be difficult.

Lack of Communication

By far, one of the greatest sources of stress for educators that is linked to administration is lack of communication. When communication in a school is effective and honest, most employees feel that they play an important role in accomplishing the institution's objectives. The communications system within an organization affects employee morale and may increase or decrease job stress. Studies have shown that when an agency improves its internal communications system, it realizes a higher level of morale among its employees (Yoder & Heneman, 1958).

Good communications within a school, a college, or an educational system can promote loyalty, establish priorities, ensure consistency, promote teamwork, provide a means for expressing ideas, clarify concerns, and motivate people. When communication is weak, these things deteriorate and everyone within the organization suffers. A weak communications system results in rumors and leaves too much to guesswork and individual interpretation. It leads practitioners to question administrative decisions. It causes job stress.

The "Catch-All" Cause

Because almost every aspect of education is affected in some way by administration, it is easy to blame the agency's or system's management when things are not going as well as hoped. For example, Truch (1980) identifies the following primary sources of teacher job dissatisfaction: 1) low salaries, 2) poor staff relations, 3) poor physical facilities, 4) burdensome teaching load, 5) inadequate teacher training, 6) large classes, 7) feelings of inadequacy as a teacher, 8) lack of preparation time, and 9) the low status of the profession within the society. Most of these can, in some way, be directly attributed to administration. For example, it is the administration that determines how much or little inservice training is provided to teachers as well as the subject matter of the instruction. Some of this blame may be well placed. Some of the ills of the profession, however, are not related to administration and management. By its nature, though, administration remains a catch-all for blame.

The stress related to management is compounded by the fact that some administrators in the field of education are not trained career managers. Rather, they are educators who received their exposure and orientation to management from the administrators who went before them. Having been educators, they are often torn between their allegiance to their former peers and the demands of administration. Although there is some merit to selecting and hiring administrators from the ranks of teachers, it may prohibit implementation of certain managerial techniques and functions. Such administrators lack some of the tools necessary to function with total effectiveness in the administrative area (Mercer & Koester, 1978). This compounds the stress related to administration.

STRIVING TOWARD ADMINISTRATION

The fact that most administrators in education are educators themselves is the basis for another category of stress. Some educators pursue administrative positions because they offer upward mobility, that is, increased status and wages. They may not genuinely want to leave classroom teaching but see no alternatives.

Having practitioners pursue positions in management to seek upward mobility is common in the human service fields. This concept raises several questions. Are the qualifications for administrative positions in education adequate to meet the demands of management? Does an educational system that requires its practitioners to look toward administration as a means for obtaining upward mobility do a disservice to both its teachers and administrators? Does a good classroom teacher make a good administrator? Must an administrator have classroom experience to perform effectively within the system? These are but a few of the questions resulting from the system of selecting administrators that exist in most school systems. It places particular stress on administrators, potential administrators, and teachers.

SUMMARY

The complexities of administration and management in education are numerous and intricate. It is an area of extreme importance to the success of any school or educational system. The relationship between administrators and teachers, though, is a primary source of stress to both groups.

Most educational systems are bureaucracies. As such, administratively oriented tasks abound. Most people cope with the administrative demands of their educational system in one of five ways. They cope as loyal servants who deal with their jobs through passive compliance. They may be angry prisoners who cope through passive resistance. Some are stress fugitives who seek to escape from potential stress on the job. Others are job reformers who regularly crusade for change within their school or system. Or, they may be stress managers who work to identify and control their job stress. Most people float from one coping technique to another, although the stress managers have the best handle on dealing with day-to-day job stress.

Administrative stressors range from tangible concerns such as work schedules to intangible concerns such as inconsistencies among supervisors and communication systems. The most frequently cited categories of stress related to administration and management are:

1. Policies and procedures
2. Work schedules
3. Relationship with supervisors, principals, and administrators
4. Inconsistency among supervisors, principals, and peers
5. Accountability for decisions made under pressure
6. Response to complaints by parents
7. Evaluation systems
8. Organizational rumors

9. Lack of physical resources
10. Standardized tests
11. Dress codes
12. Work overload
13. Budget and fiscal support
14. Public scrutiny
15. Collective bargaining
16. Teacher strikes
17. Change
18. Lack of communication

When stress becomes excessive, educators experience job discontentment. The administration of the school or educational system is generally blamed. In some cases, the blame is well placed. In others, it is not. Generally, though, by its nature, administration is a "catch-all" for blame in causing stress in education.

Stress is also inherent in how educational administrators are selected. It exists for those educators who aspire to administration. This is due, in part, to the fact that administration offers one of the few forms of upward mobility available to educators. While some aspire to administrative positions as a result of conscious career planning, others simply wish to advance in status and wages.

Administrative matters must be addressed by every member of the educational system, from principal to classroom teacher to secretary, every day. Administrative concerns involve directing and managing people, things, and activities. While sometimes cumbersome and stressful, administrative tasks are essential to the effective functioning of an organization, agency, or system.

Even though many of the administrative aspects of education are common to other human service fields and many private businesses, there are many that are unique. As such, they create unusual stress, strain, and tension for the members of the system.

REFERENCES

Anderson, L., & Van Dyke, L. *Secondary school administration.* New York: Houghton Mifflin Co., 1972.

Girdano, D., & Everly, G. *Controlling stress and tension.* Englewood Cliffs, N J: Prentice-Hall, 1979.

Levinson, H. *Executive stress.* New York: Harper & Row, 1970.

Mercer, J. L., & Koester, E. H. *Public management systems.* New York: American Management Association, 1978.

Phelps, L. *Police tasks and related stress factors: From an organizational perspective.* Reno: University of Nevada Press, 1977.

Toffler, A. *Future shock.* New York: Bantam Books, Inc., 1970.

Truch, S. *Teacher burnout.* Novato, CA: Academic Therapy Publications, 1980.

Veninga, R. L., & Spradley, J. P. *The work-stress connection: How to cope with job burnout.* New York: Ballantine Books, Inc., 1981.

Wilson, O. *Police administration.* New York: McGraw-Hill Book Co., 1977.

Yoder, D., & Heneman, H. *Handbook of personnel management and labor relations.* New York: McGraw-Hill Book Co., 1958.

Chapter 7

Home, Family, and Social Life
Compounding Stress in Education

The personal life of a teacher—at home, with family, or socially—can be a haven from the daily stresses and strains associated with education. It can offer an escape from the daily grind. Conversely, home, family, and social life can compound and add to the stresses of the workday. The influence of home, family, friends, and social or leisure activities on stress is unparalleled. The stresses and strains of life are compounded when these invaluable support systems break down.

EFFECTS OF HOME, FAMILY, AND SOCIAL LIFE ON THE JOB

When relationships with loved ones are good, a strong supportive circle of friends exists, and things at home are functioning smoothly, an educator is in a good position to cope with the stresses and strains associated with the job. The positive support provided by family, friends, and a comfortable home life is invaluable. A home life that consists of turmoil, conflict, and anxiety will compound job stress. The tensions of private life will generally spill over into the workday. Leaving the tensions of a stressful home and family situation behind is difficult, if not impossible.

A person's family has unlimited potential for being either a source of relief from stress and strain or a source of stress itself. Most people recognize that excessive stress in the home and with family is disruptive and affects life on the job. Few educators can completely separate themselves from the stresses and strains of home and family simply because they've entered their school building or office.

Traditionally, an educator's family and home are sources of understanding, acceptance, support, compassion, and love. The nature of family relationships determines whether they truly meet this ideal. All families suffer some strain some of the time. But when tension and worry within the family run high, the negative effects of stress will be realized (Yates, 1979). Inevitably, the stress will be carried forth to the workplace, whether it be an elementary classroom, an administrative office, or a college campus.

Some Conflict in All Families

Some tension, turmoil, misunderstanding, insensitivities, and problems exist in every family and every close friendship. The closest of families will experience some arguments, dissension, and tension among its members. Minor tensions and conflicts occur almost everyday.

All people possess unique characteristics. Their traits set them apart from others, make them special, and attract others to them. Being different from one another, conflicts will occur. However, most people grow as a result of day-to-day conflicts.

It is nearly impossible for educators to prevent family situations from having some impact on their job (Yates, 1979). A child with the flu, an argument before breakfast, and a lost pet may send a person to work feeling tense and irritable.

The Holmes and Rahe Social Readjustment Rating (see Chapter 8 for an in-depth discussion) is a stress indicator, identifying many family and social life events as negative stressors. Included are such items as marital reconciliation, trouble with in-laws, change in church activities, change in social activities, sex difficulties, and vacation. The impact of each can be significant. Collectively, their impact on a person's professional life is inevitable. Similarly, the collective strains and tensions that occur on the job may affect life at home.

PERSONAL GOALS AND CONFLICT

Almost everyone has personal goals. People's goals may range from obtaining great wealth to developing athletic prowess. They may include serving people in need, living a quiet life in a small country town, or making a significant and lasting change in the field of education.

A person who has developed a good set of life goals will generally strike a balance between those that can be practically achieved and those that are more distant. The goals provide motivation and momentum for the person. They challenge an individual to tax his or her potential. They are often shared with family and friends, and, once reached, provide a sense of accomplishment and self-worth. Well-established goals provide direction for an individual's personal and professional life.

Goals may be established for professional advancement, skills enhancement, financial growth, obtaining particular possessions, achieving status within the community, and providing for the well-being of others. There is personal reward in achieving goals. However, if goals are not realized, a person may feel hindered, defeated, frustrated, or tense.

Selye (1974) states that people's long-term and short-term aims or goals may be divided into four groups. They include:

1. Leaning on the powerful—This includes such goals as pleasing God, serving a person's country, and promoting the good of the family through self-sacrifice. It also includes maintaining a personal code of honor.
2. Being powerful—This group of aims includes seeking fame, recognition, and status symbols. It also includes gaining a sense of job and personal security.
3. Giving joy—This group is particularly important to educators. It involves such aims as serving others without ulterior motives, giving gifts and charity, creating art, loving animals, and more.
4. Getting joy—Included in this group are such life aims as seeking pleasure and self-gratification. These may be pursued through sex, food, drink, travel, and the passive enjoyment of art.

A teacher whose goals include implementing a new curriculum, helping several students who are having difficulties, and pursuing advancement to department head or team leader will grow anxious if the goals are not realized within his or her projected time plan. If the teacher experiences another period or two in which goals are not realized, self-doubt and/or anger directed at the school system may develop. Ultimately, the teacher who is continuously frustrated in his or her attempts to accomplish goals may resign. When the job interferes with personal or family goals, such as purchasing a nice home or having more time to spend with friends, frustration will mount. Selye (1974) points out that one of the major sources of distress among people engaged in the most common occupations in modern society is dissatisfaction with life resulting from disrespect for their own accomplishments.

DEDICATION TO FAMILY

When conflict occurs between job and family, stress will occur. As stated, an educator's goal may be to spend more time with family. If the demands of the job are too great, spending time with family and friends may be difficult. If the teacher's family then makes additional demands for time, conflict occurs. The educator plays a game of tug-of-war between family and the profession.

Stress may also be experienced if the educator's family is not familiar enough with the profession to provide needed support and understanding. For any human service practitioner, a strong, supportive home environment is invaluable. When this support system does not exist, the tensions and anxieties of the workday mount.

Stress may increase if the educator's work causes inconvenience to family members. When the family's needs are not met because of the job, anger toward the profession may evolve among its members. Children may ask why their parent's work is taking up so much time. The educator's spouse may have no patience for explanations of the importance of individualized instruction or learning styles. This becomes particularly stressful for the educator who feels trapped between dedication to the job and dedication to the family. As one educator's wife remarked, "I don't think I will ever have to worry about his going through a mid-life crisis, getting sick, or seeking another woman. He doesn't have the time."

Family stress may be compounded if more than one person works outside of the home. Both husband and wife devote time to their professions. Both seek support from family and spouse at the end of a difficult workday. But time once allocated to family may be given up to work-related tasks. It is difficult to avoid stress when family and separate professions tug at both household members for time and energy.

Dr. David Torbett, Director of the Family Enrichment Foundation in Denver, Colorado, believes the demands being placed on families today are both external and internal. The internal ones are those resulting from the emotional interaction within the family. The external ones are those resulting from communication, the effects of jobs on the family members, and the strains of financial obligations. The family is also influenced by the pressures of today's mechanistic society that place too great an emphasis on production and achievement and too little emphasis on expression of human feelings (Forbes, 1979).

SOCIAL ACTIVITIES

Social activities can cause stress. If the job interferes with social functions, a person experiences the negative effects of stress. The same is true when social activities interfere with job-related tasks.

There is no link between volume of work and leisure. The balance between work and leisure is personal and individuals generally function so that there is a healthy mixture of both. When work or leisure consumes too much of a person's time, however, negative stress will develop.

Just as stress exists on the job, it is inherent in most leisure activities. For example, the Holmes and Rahe Social Readjustment Rating Scale lists vacation as a source of stress. Selye (1974) notes that it is not the type or the amount of work or leisure that causes stress. Rather, it is the quality that matters. He points out that too much leisure can be harmful. The best leisure is realized when a person is tired as a result of his or her work, much the same as a good meal is most enjoyable when a person is genuinely hungry.

There are certain stressors within a teacher's social life that may create tension regardless of the balance struck between work and leisure. For example, it is common for educators to socialize with other educators. They understand one another and share many of the same professional and personal concerns. However, this type of socializing does not always allow for true leisure, that is, escaping from the workday. Instead, interaction with other educators in a social setting may add to the emotional and mental strains already carried home from the job.

Socializing may be stressful for educators whose job follows them to leisure functions. No sooner do they arrive at a party, for example, before people begin talking about the problems their children are having in school. Someone will inevitably approach the teacher and levy an opinion on the value of today's educational system.

There are also job-related social activities in which educators are expected to participate. Student performances, athletic competitions, open houses, and other student activities must be attended. When these occur to excess or interfere with other functions that the educator would like to attend, he or she will grow increasingly distressed.

FINANCES

Money matters are responsible for a great deal of personal anguish. Keeping up with the Joneses and living beyond one's means are common philosophies in personal financial management. Financial difficulties are particularly stressful because they are very personal. They are often associated with a person's ego and self-esteem.

Most educators entered the field knowing that they would never attain great wealth. Despite this, they may experience stress when they see other people who have the same or less job preparation earning much more. They may also feel tense over the uncertain fiscal future of their educational system as they read about layoffs in systems throughout the country. Many educators moonlight to earn extra money, creating additional stress in the form of time away from family, fatigue, and anxiety in dealing with a second set of employers, rules, and peers.

JOB SECURITY

Closely related to finances as a cause of stress is job security. In education, as stated earlier, many systems are being forced to lay off teachers. Declining student enrollments and lack of fiscal resources are the primary reasons given. This situation has created concern among most educators who once felt quite secure in their positions.

When a person feels insecure in his or her employment, it will generally have an effect on family members, friends, and co-workers. The educator may feel that he or she has to do more than the next person in order to prove his or her worth. Educators may turn their insecurity into anger toward the system, growing discontent and attacking the system at every opportunity.

People need to feel secure in their work. When they do not, they will be affected by stress physically, mentally, and emotionally, which will have an impact on family and home life. It is widely accepted that feelings of job insecurity do not drive a person to work more productively but, rather, put the person under so much stress that he or she works at a far less effective rate. For example, a teacher who fears layoff due to budgetary cutbacks will not perform more effectively in order to convince the administration to keep him or her on the job. Instead, feelings of insecurity, depression, and futility may lead to reduced performance. Studies indicate that in such circumstances, people tend to spend more of their time with co-workers, lamenting their potential fate and discussing who will be laid off first. Psychologists such as Abraham Maslow have cited the importance of a sense of job security as a minimal condition for productivity in the workplace (Yates, 1979).

EDUCATION

For educators, pursuing additional education may be another source of stress. Many school systems, colleges, and universities require that their teachers and administrators pursue advanced education. In some states, advanced education is required to maintain teacher certification. Some public school teachers, for example, must obtain an advanced degree within a specified period of time in order to receive an increase in wages.

Education is an excellent stress reducer. It provides mental stimulation and new skills for the student. It provides opportunity for interaction with new people and may serve as a welcomed escape from daily routine. However, when advanced education is required and interferes with family and other pursuits, its positive effects may not be realized. Courses may take time that would otherwise be spent with family. Meeting demands such as completing papers and studying for exams may create new stress for the educator and his or her family members.

The strain of learning may take its toll like any other stressor. It may be compounded if the school system, college, or university that required the pursuit does not have an adequate reward system to recognize educational achievement. If the school or state regulation requires advanced education but does not provide tuition reimbursement or some other financial assistance, additional stress will be realized.

Educational pursuits may also cause stress for the educators who want to attend seminars and workshops to enhance their knowledge and skills. If the school does not provide the time or financial assistance necessary to attend these programs, the educator may pursue them on weekends or in the evening and with his or her own funds. Again, the anxiety and frustration that may result will affect both the educator and his or her family.

MAINTAINING GOOD HEALTH

There is a direct link between physical health and stress. For some educators, stress is experienced because demands of the job and family do not allow them to pursue good personal health. For example, a teacher may go to school and spend a long day in front of the classroom even though he or she is ill. In order to continue to provide needed services to students, the teacher may put off taking care of illnesses such as viruses, hypertension, backache, and stomach ailments.

Illness may be the result of highly stressful events that occur during the educator's workday or within the home. Medical studies have shown that highly emotional and tense situations may lead to an increase in susceptibility to illnesses such as headache, backache, and infectious disease (Simonton, 1978).

The sick-leave system that exists for the educator may either reduce or compound the stress. If the system provides adequate opportunity for the teacher or administrator to take off to cope with an illness, the stress level will be reduced. If it is excessively complex or if the educator is made to feel guilty for using sick leave, stress will increase.

A job hazard inherent in education is the exposure to illness that a teacher or administrator experiences. Every day, the classroom teacher interacts with students who may be carrying any number of diseases and illnesses. It is common for an illness to affect large numbers of students and teachers in a school. The teacher may then transmit the illness to family members at home.

SELFLESS IMAGE

The selfless image of the educator has an impact on family members. Many people see educators as people who are always willing to serve. Their personal and family needs should, in the minds of many, take a backseat to the needs of students and their school. They are viewed as giving, selfless people with no limit on the time and energy they are willing to give.

A selfless image is not necessarily stressful. It may be an important part of a person's self-concept. It may be a source of pride. When it interferes with family life or interaction with friends, it may become stressful. If the selfless image is carried to excess, stress develops. If there is no relationship between an educator's selfless image and satisfaction on the job, that is, the selflessness is not recognized or rewarded, stress develops.

SUMMARY

An educator's home, family, and social life can be a source of relief from the stresses and strains associated with the job. Good personal relationships and a comfortable home life make coping with tension and strain on the job and in other life experiences easier. Thus, they can be valuable support systems. On the other hand, an educator's home, family, and social life may also compound job stress. If an educator's home and social life is filled with turmoil, conflict, and anxiety, this can spill over into the classroom. The influence of home life on stress levels is unparalleled.

Some conflict exists in all families and among close friends. This is due, in part, to the unique personalities of the individuals. When conflicts become excessive, stress develops. Holmes and Rahe, in their Social Readjustment Rating Scale, cite numerous stress indicators relating directly to home, family, and social life.

Personal goals are important to the increase or reduction of stress. Well-developed goals will motivate a person toward professional and personal growth. When a person has clear short-range and long-range direction in his or her life, the path of the future is easier to travel. However, the goals or direction must be realistic. If not, they may compound rather than reduce stress. To have job satisfaction, a person needs to know that her or his professional goals may be realized.

Stress evolves when there is repeated conflict between the demands of the education profession and the demands made by family and home life. Time is one of the major areas of conflict, as the job requires that work often be done at home and that meetings and conferences be attended after normal work hours. Selye (1974) points out that it is not the volume of work or leisure that is harmful to an individual but, rather, the quality of work and leisure-time activities.

Social activities may compound job stress. For example, the teacher who is approached by someone at a party who wants assistance in helping a child get better grades may grow frustrated at not being able to escape the job. There may also be social activities at which the educator's presence is expected such as student dances or athletic events. The educator may have other desires, but these must be put aside.

Financial matters may cause stress. Educators will not attain great wealth through their involvement in the educational system. Many of their desires may not be realized. Finances are often linked to self-esteem. When desires are not met due to lack of finances, a person's self-esteem may be lowered. Finances may also be a source of conflict within the family. When these things occur, stress mounts.

For an employee to feel comfortable in a job, he or she must have a sense of job security. In education, fiscal constraints and declining enrollments have caused some educators to question their job security. When a person feels insecure at work, the dissatisfaction that results will generally be carried into the home and will ultimately affect family members.

Many systems require their educators to pursue advanced education. Some require advanced degrees within a specific time period in order for the educator to gain a salary increase. While some systems have liberal tuition reimbursement programs, some do not. This places an additional burden on the educator. In addition, the time that goes into preparing lessons and studying affects everyone in the family. If the support system for the educator is good, the pursuit of advanced education can be an excellent stress reducer.

Maintaining good health may also cause stress. Many educators will work when ill because of their sense of obligation to their students. Others will contract illness and disease within the school, as a result of interacting with so many other people, and will transmit it to family members. Educators will also contract illnesses that are directly associated with job stress, such as infectious disease, backache, and stomach ailments. The sick-leave system provided to educators may hinder recovery. If it is overly complex or if the educator is made to feel guilty for using sick leave, the system may be a source of stress.

The image of the educator as a selfless, giving worker is both good and bad. It may be a positive and important part of the person's self-image. It may also be a strain as people expect dedication to the field to take precedence over personal and family demands. The positive and negative aspects of the image are shared by family members.

The educator's profession is not one that can be begun at 9:00 A.M. and ended at 5:00 P.M., Monday through Friday. It places special demands on the individual. Involvement in the profession requires performing tasks at home. The profession also exposes the educator to certain stressors that also affect family and friends. These include low to moderate wages, exposure to a variety of illnesses within the school, and demand for attendance at job-related functions during nonwork hours. Most families adjust well to the profession. Others find it quite stressful. Through implementation of some of the stress-management techniques provided in this text, some of the strain on family members may be reduced.

REFERENCES

Forbes,R. *Life stress.* New York: Doubleday & Co., 1979.

Greenberg, S. F., & Valletutti, P. J. *Stress and the helping professions.* Baltimore: Paul H. Brookes Publishing Co., 1980.

Selye, H. *The stress of life.* New York: McGraw-Hill Book Co, 1974.

Simonton, C. *Getting well again.* Los Angeles: J. P. Tarcher, Inc., 1978.

Yates, J. *Managing stress.* New York: American Management Association, 1979.

Chapter 8

Understanding
Risk Factors

Understanding the risk factors related to negative stress is of particular importance to human service professionals. Like any disease, if caught early, the likelihood of resolution is enhanced. There is no substitute for early detection of problems and timely implementation of appropriate cure.

Every educator should be able to determine his or her own stress level. Hundreds of self-evaluation and self-help assessments are available at local libraries. Most physicians can provide a summary of a person's stress level during a routine physical examination.

RISK FACTORS

The majority of the self-help tests and quizzes are designed to measure risk factors. There is rarely a single cause of stress, and measuring risk factors generally provides an overview of an individual's total situation. For example, a cardiologist rarely considers a single cause when examining a person who has had a heart attack. The doctor considers general physical well-being, personal habits, work environment, family situation, heredity, and much more. The doctor seeks out a group of causal factors that ultimately led to the attack and then prescribes treatment that includes reduction or elimination of the causes. A teacher who smokes heavily, is overweight, feels strained by classroom teaching, and has a tense family situation may be a classic candidate for heart disease.

Risk factors generally work in combination. It is unusual to find a single risk factor causing severe problems, although it is possible. In considering potential for heart disease, for example, an educator should consider the following primary risk factors:

1. High cholesterol level
2. High blood pressure or hypertension
3. Cigarette smoking
4. Overweight
5. Lack of exercise
6. Overexertion
7. Advanced age
8. Family history of heart disease
9. Insufficient vitamin B_6
10. Stress (Veninga & Spradley, 1981)

A teacher or school administrator who wants to assess her or his stress level will generally give consideration to three broad areas: psychosocial, bioecological, and personality. The psychosocial level includes the interaction between social behavior and how the person interprets that behavior. It addresses many day-to-day events and the value a person gives to them. The psychosocial areas shows the various interpretations people will give to the same event or activity. The bioecological area focuses on the individual's physical characteristics and his or her relationship with the environment. Exposure to noise, which is commonplace for many teachers, is a bioecological cause of stress. The third area, personality, addresses an individual's self-perception, attitudes, and general behavior and how they affect daily functioning and stress reactions (Girdano & Everly, 1979). These areas are measured in most of the self-assessment devices available.

SOCIAL READJUSTMENT RATING SCALE

One of the classic self-assessment tools is the Holmes and Rahe Social Readjustment Rating Scale (Table 1). Developed in 1967, this scale assigns a numeric value or weight to a particular life event based on the amount of stress attributed to it. Holmes and Rahe, of the University of Washington, identified 43 life events based on work with over 5,000 people. They identified both positive and negative stressors in the scale. Positive events such as marriage, a business adjustment, and a change in church activities were given point values on the scale because each requires some degree of readjustment (Holmes & Rahe, 1967). A point value is given for each event on the scale. A person taking the assessment should record the point values for each event that has taken place in his or her life during the past 12 months. The point value follows each item. The point values for applicable items should be added to provide a total score. The scale has proved to be an effective indicator of susceptibility to stress-related illness. Individuals who accumulate the highest scores are generally most susceptible. A high score does not necessarily mean that the individual will definitely become ill, since people react differently to stress. A "high" score is obtained

Table 1. The Holmes and Rahe Social Readjustment
Rating Scale

Life event	Mean value
Death of spouse	100
Divorce	73
Marital separation	65
Jail term	63
Death of close family member	63
Personal injury or illness	53
Marriage	50
Fired from work	47
Marital reconciliation	45
Retirement	45
Change in family member's health	44
Pregnancy	40
Sex difficulties	39
Addition to family	39
Business readjustment	39
Change in financial status	38
Death of close friend	37
Change to different line of work	36
Change in number of marital arguments	35
Mortgage or loan over $10,000	31
Foreclosure of mortgage or loan	30
Change in work responsibilities	29
Son or daughter leaving home	29
Trouble with in-laws	29
Outstanding personal achievement	28
Spouse begins or stops work	26
Starting or finishing school	26
Change in living conditions	25
Revision of personal habits	24
Trouble with boss	23
Change in work hours, conditions	20
Change in residence	20
Change in schools	20
Change in recreational habits	19
Change in church activities	19
Change in social activities	18
Mortgage or loan under $10,000	17

(continued)

Table 1. (*Continued*)

Life event	Mean value
Change in sleeping habits	16
Change in number of family gatherings	15
Change in eating habits	15
Vacation	13
Christmas season	12
Minor violations of the law	11

when point values total to 300 or more points. A "low" score is a total point value of 150 or fewer points. A "moderate" score is any total falling between the two extremes (Girdano & Everly, 1979).

Yates points out that a person scoring 150 or fewer points has a 33% chance of experiencing a serious health change over the coming year. An individual scoring 150 to 300 points increases that chance to 50%. A person accumulating more than 300 points has an 80%–90% chance of experiencing an illness (Yates, 1979).

Not all scales that are designed to measure risk are based on point values. The following series of questions is designed to measure the degree of harmful tension and anxiety a person is experiencing. The person taking the assessment need only answer the questions with "sometimes" or "frequently."

1. Do you get irritable over petty things?
2. Does your irritability turn into uncontrollable anger?
3. Are you becoming hypercritical of others?
4. Do you feel increasingly sorry for yourself?
5. Are you too busy to eat?
6. Do you have trouble falling asleep?
7. Do you have trouble staying asleep?
8. Are you too tired to think?
9. Are you a nonstop talker?
10. Do you find it difficult to converse?
11. Must you be first in everything?
12. Do minor disappointments throw you?
13. Do you find you have too much to do and too little time to do it in?
14. Are you unable to stop worrying?
15. Are you bored?
16. Do you feel neglected, left out?
17. Do you feel you are indispensable?
18. Do you feel trapped?

19. Do you feel as if you want to run away?
20. Are you anxious about the future?
21. Do your hands tremble?
22. Do you laugh or cry uncontrollably?
23. Do you worry about aches and pains?
24. Are you conscious of the beating of your heart?
25. Do you perspire excessively under the arms?
26. Is your stomach queasy?
27. Do you have pains in your stomach?
28. Do you suffer from dizzy spells?
29. Do you need a tranquilizer or drink before facing a meeting or a decision?

The above questions simply point to a person's susceptibility to stress-related illness and disorder. The person who answers "sometimes" to some of the questions may simply be responding to the environment at a given time. Educators who answer "frequently" to a number of the questions may be suffering from excessive tension and anxiety (Winter, 1976). For example, an elementary or high school teacher who does not sleep well, eats poorly, worries a great deal, is overly critical, and suffers stomach or muscular pains on a regular basis is probably a candidate for succumbing to the many negative effects of stress.

STRESS DIAGNOSTIC SURVEY # 1

Organizational Stressors

Risk factors caused by a job or an organization may also be measured using self-help devices. The following quiz provides an indication of the impact of job stress as it relates to organizational stressors. A person taking the quiz should place a corresponding number from the following scale before each item to best describe the source of stress.

1 = Never a source of stress
2 = Rarely a source of stress
3 = Occasionally a source of stress
4 = Sometimes a source of stress
5 = Often a source of stress
6 = Usually a source of stress
7 = Always a source of stress

_____ 1. The red tape to accomplish my job is significant.
_____ 2. I have little control over my work.
_____ 3. Frequent changes are made in the organization.
_____ 4. I have no privacy.
_____ 5. My supervisor doesn't respect me.
_____ 6. The reports that I must read or complete are growing in number.

_____ 7. We follow no formal authority system around here.

_____ 8. People come and go regularly—here today, gone tomorrow.

_____ 9. I am not prepared to work with other departments or people from other units.

_____10. My supervisor doesn't trust me.

_____11. I have little say in decisions that affect my work.

_____12. The organization is too formal and stiff—impersonal.

_____13. Changes are declared and put into place without any input from people at my level.

_____14. I have no control over what is happening in my work area (office, work station, desk).

_____15. My supervisor is unpredictable—what he or she will do next is a mystery (Matteson & Ivancevich, 1982).

Generally, items with scores of one or two represent low stress, scores of three or four represent moderate stress, scores of five or six represent high stress, and scores of seven represent dangerous stress. The following two surveys use the same scoring scale. Once completed, an educator can determine which of the stress categories (organizational, group, or job and career categories) is appropriate based on the total number of low, moderate, high, and dangerous scores listed. An educator who sees his or her supervisor infrequently, is uncertain about how to channel a problem through the chain of authority, and is regularly upset by new rules or decisions may already be a victim of stress-related disorders.

STRESS DIAGNOSTIC SURVEY # 2

Group Stressors

The following survey focuses on stress and risk factors as they relate to group interaction on the job. Again, an educator taking this survey should use the scale cited above.

_____1. I am not able to keep up with my group's performance.

_____2. I am not a member of a close-knit group.

_____3. I receive no support for my personal goals from my group.

_____4. I don't know what my group wants from me.

_____5. My work group has no clout in the organization.

_____6. I receive no sense of security from my group affiliation.

_____7. I fear being kicked out of my group.

_____8. My work group is disorganized and cold.

_____9. I don't get a sense of social satisfaction from my group (Matteson & Ivancevich, 1982).

STRESS DIAGNOSTIC SURVEY # 3

Job and Career Stressors

The following survey deals with job and career stressors. The numbered scale from above should be used.

_____ 1. I work on many unnecessary job activities.

_____ 2. My job objectives are unclear to me.

_____ 3. To keep up with my job, I usually have to take work home.

_____ 4. My job is boring.

_____ 5. I am responsible for people.

_____ 6. My job pushes me hard to finish on time.

_____ 7. My work area (office space) is too crowded.

_____ 8. I do not have enough opportunities to advance in this organization.

_____ 9. I have job activities that are accepted by one person but not by others.

_____10. I do not have the authority to do my job well.

_____11. My job is too difficult.

_____12. My job has become too routine.

_____13. I must make decisions that affect the career, safety, or lives of other people.

_____14. There is not enough time in the day to do my job.

_____15. Work conditions on the job are below par.

_____16. I am at a standstill in my career.

_____17. I receive conflicting requests from two or more poeple.

_____18. I am not sure of what is expected of me.

_____19. I am responsible for too many jobs.

_____20. My job is too easy.

_____21. I am responsible for helping others solve their problems and difficulties.

_____22. I don't have time to take an occasional break from the job.

_____23. My working conditions are not as good as those of others.

_____24. I am in a career that offers little promise for the future.

The self-help surveys and quizzes listed above represent only a small sample of those available to educators in helping them to understand their risk factors and the level of stress to which they are exposed every day. Teachers and administrators taking them should remember that they are only indicators. Their accuracy will not be the same for all people and they will never replace a detailed physical examination by a physician as a stress-measurement device.

TYPE "A" VERSUS TYPE "B"

Two cardiologists, Friedman and Rosenman, conducted research over a period of 20 years in the areas of heart disease, personality, and behavior. They concluded that a person who is considered to have a Type "A" personality is two or three times more likely to develop coronary heart disease than someone who is considered to be Type "B."

Typically, a teacher or administrator with Type "A" personality is one who has a chronic sense of time urgency and feels he or she must accomplish as much as possible in as little time as possible. The Type "A" personality is also very competitive and may be aggressive. He or she usually has some sort of undirected, possibly hostile energy lying dormant, waiting to be aroused.

> Type "A" behavior pattern is an action–emotion complex that can be observed in any person who is aggressively involved in a chronic, incessant struggle to achieve more and more in less and less time, and if required to do so, against the opposing efforts of other things or other persons. It is not psychosis or a complex of worries or fears of phobias or obsessions, but a socially acceptable—indeed often praised—form of conflict. Persons possessing this pattern also are quite prone to exhibit a free-floating but extraordinarily well-rationalized hostility. As might be expected, there are degrees in the intensity of this behavior pattern (Friedman & Rosenman, 1974).

Type "B" personalities have many of the same qualities as Type "A" personalities; however, their characteristics are not as chronic or incessant. Some authorities believe that approximately one-half of the American population consists of Type "A" personalities. This is due, in part, to the society and the socioeconomic system that reward many of the values associated with Type "A" personality (Yates, 1979). For example, most people in the field of education think highly of the teacher who is always "on the go," involved in meetings, volunteering for extra assignments, and constantly working at home. Few would view this as negative, possibly harmful behavior. In fact, it may be rewarded or reinforced.

Most people possess some characteristics of Type "A" and Type "B" personalities. However, one is usually dominant. Type "A" behavior does not necessarily brand a person doomed to a life of heart disease. In fact, some people function well as Type "A" personalities. For them, to slow down completely would cause more strain and anxiety than it would resolve, so long as they are not pushed beyond their limits. With regard to medical findings, though, a person with a dominant Type "A" behavior would be well advised to slow down his or her hectic life-style.

The following questionnaire will assist a person in determining the extent to which he or she has Type "A" behavior. The person completing the questionnaire should use a rating scale of 0–10, with "0" being extremely low, "5" being average, and "10" being extremely high.

_____ 1. To what extent do you hurry the ends of a sentence or explosively accentuate key words even when there is no real need to do so?

_____ 2. To what extent do you always move, walk, and eat rapidly?

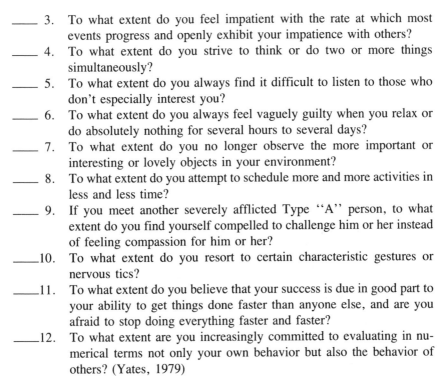

_____ 3. To what extent do you feel impatient with the rate at which most events progress and openly exhibit your impatience with others?

_____ 4. To what extent do you strive to think or do two or more things simultaneously?

_____ 5. To what extent do you always find it difficult to listen to those who don't especially interest you?

_____ 6. To what extent do you always feel vaguely guilty when you relax or do absolutely nothing for several hours to several days?

_____ 7. To what extent do you no longer observe the more important or interesting or lovely objects in your environment?

_____ 8. To what extent do you attempt to schedule more and more activities in less and less time?

_____ 9. If you meet another severely afflicted Type "A" person, to what extent do you find yourself compelled to challenge him or her instead of feeling compassion for him or her?

_____10. To what extent do you resort to certain characteristic gestures or nervous tics?

_____11. To what extent do you believe that your success is due in good part to your ability to get things done faster than anyone else, and are you afraid to stop doing everything faster and faster?

_____12. To what extent are you increasingly committed to evaluating in numerical terms not only your own behavior but also the behavior of others? (Yates, 1979)

Ratings of higher than 60 indicate a Type "A" personality. But, the adage "know thyself" must prevail. The individual is the best judge in determining his or her behavior patterns and the harm they may be causing.

SUMMARY

In judging one's self, honesty must be emphasized and the tendency to be overly critical must be avoided. The preliminary step in coping with and reducing stress is recognizing when stress is occurring and when a certain behavior sets a foundation on which stress can grow. The mistake many educators make is in judging themselves too harshly. When this occurs, they either become discouraged about the potential for reducing and managing stress because the task appears too awesome, or the results of their self-evaluation create added stress.

A wide variety of self-evaluation tests and quizzes are available for educators to use in measuring their current stress levels and potential for succumbing to the harmful effects of stress. Most are located in texts on the subject of stress, found in local libraries. Almost all of the available assessments are simply indicators and their results are rarely conclusive. They serve only as guides for teachers, administrators, and others in the field of education to use in making personal judgments.

In the following chapter, specific stress symptoms are cited. In addition, classic warning signs are provided. The same advice that was offered for self-assessment devices, i.e., avoid harsh judgments and give honest, careful consideration to personal behavior patterns, should be followed when studying the symptoms of stress.

REFERENCES

Friedman, M., & Rosenman, R. *Type A behavior and your heart.* New York: Alfred A. Knopf, Inc., 1974.

Girdano, D. & Everly, G. *Controlling stress and tension.* Englewood Cliffs, N.J.: Prentice-Hall, 1979.

Holmes, T., & Rahe, R. The social readjustment rating scale. *Journal of Psychosomatic Research,* 1967, *11,* 213–218.

Matteson, & Ivancevich. *Managing job stress and health: The intelligent person's guide.* New York: The Free Press, 1982.

Veninga, R. L., & Spradley, J. P. *The work-stress connection: How to cope with job burnout.* New York: Ballantine Books, Inc., 1981.

Winter, R. *Triumph over tension.* New York: Grosset & Dunlap, 1976.

Yates, J. *Managing stress.* New York: American Management Association, 1979.

Chapter 9

Identifying Symptoms

The importance of being able to identify the symptoms of negative stress or distress cannot be understated. Identifying the symptoms of stress is as important to stress management as identifying the symptoms of an infection or flu is to the ultimate cure. Identifying the symptoms of stress is no more difficult than identifying the symptoms of the most common illnesses, that is, once they are learned.

While the need for stress-awareness programs has been recognized in many businesses and industries, there are few programs offered to employees in the human service fields. In the field of education, workshops and seminars have been provided to employees on a haphazard basis. In some systems, faculty and staff have been exposed to occasional instructional programs on the topic. In other systems, no programs have been offered to employees.

TRAITS OF A STRESS-PRONE PERSON

Forbes (1979) identified some basic traits or characteristics of a stress-prone person. The list is intended to serve as a guide for educators to compare with their own behavior. Many of the characteristics are common among educators. There are 10 characteristics in the list. No one person will possess all of them in the same degree. A brief explanation is offered for each one.

The Tendency to Overplan Each Day

People who tend to overplan each day rarely accomplish everything they hope to in a given period of time. Their self-imposed schedule is often filled with unrealistic goals for the time allotted and, as a result, they always seem to fall behind. These people try to fit as many things as possible into the shortest amount of time. One example of such a person is a college professor who pushes herself everyday to prepare for and teach classes, write articles, conduct studies, and maintain a small consulting business. There is rarely time in the professor's schedule for family, friends, and relaxation. The times when everything is up to date are even more rare.

Polyphasic Thinking

The characteristic of polyphasic thought involves thinking about two or more things simultaneously. It is most common among people who are involved in one activity but who are thinking about several others that have to be attended to at the same time.

The nature of education imposes this characteristic on many educators. For example, a classroom teacher may be giving a lesson and thinking about the parent conference that will follow, both at the same time. People with this characteristic may eat and read at the same time, interrupt others because their thoughts are on too many things, or speak at an excessively rapid pace.

The Need to Win

To be happy, some stress-prone educators need to win. The idea of winning becomes an end in itself. Being the winner becomes an obsession, even though these people will convince themselves and others that they are excited about the challenge of succeeding. Sometimes the need to win becomes so important that a simple game with a child may become a competitive match.

Persistent Desire for Recognition

The need for recognition pervades everything done by some people who are stress-prone. While all people need recognition and advancement, the need remains reasonable and they are able to gain a sense of self-satisfaction from their successes. For people who persistently strive for recognition, there is little joy in success and accomplishment unless it is accompanied by some form of advancement. One example of this is the teacher who prepares a new lesson and hands it to his or her supervisor for review. The teacher, needing recognition immediately, will stand by the supervisor for a long period of time until the supervisor offers words of praise and acceptance. For this teacher, delayed recognition is insufficient. It must be immediate.

Inability to Relax without Feeling Guilty

One of the most common characteristics of stress-prone people is the inability to relax without feeling guilty. Such people tend to have difficulty relaxing, even in their leisure activities. The social life of these people may become burdensome because of everything that they try to accomplish. When sitting in an easy chair, for example, many educators feel guilty because they think they should be accomplishing something. Pure relaxation is difficult for them to attain. They have not struck a sound balance between work and play and, as a result, tend to have very few worthwhile hobbies or recreational pursuits.

Impatience with Delays/Interruptions

Stress-prone people have little patience for others, particularly when tasks are not being accomplished as quickly as they'd like. People with this characteristic tend to be overly critical of the way others work. They tend toward hurrying the pace of all events, whether they are professional, personal, or social.

Involvement in Multiple Projects with Many Deadlines

Parallel to some of the traits listed above, some stress-prone people will involve themselves in many, many projects and activities beyond the basic responsibility of their job. They are driven to meet deadlines and become their own worst enemy by overextending themselves. They are as involved socially and civically as they are professionally.

Chronic Sense of Time Urgency

As seen in some of the previously mentioned characteristics, stress-prone educators are in a continuous battle against time. They seem frustrated by the clock but make an effort to create a hectic and demanding pace for themselves. They are constantly striving to do more in less time. Time pressures are present in almost every aspect of their lives. As Forbes (1979) states, "they seem to live by the stop watch . . . they become slaves to time."

Excessive Competitive Drive

While competition is a way of life in modern society, stress-prone people tend to have an unhealthy approach to it. They have an almost compulsive attitude and view even routine tasks as competitions or challenges. This creates a constant restlessness and causes these people to grow increasingly more discontented. They do not seem to be satisfied as long as others have more or there is more of something to be gained.

Workaholism/Compulsion to Overwork

People tend to admire someone who has devoted himself or herself completely to the work at hand, day in and day out. As with any other of life's pursuits, though, moderation in work is important. Stress-prone educators tend to ignore many aspects of their life that do not involve their work. They are the earliest to arrive and the last to leave. They take work home and put its accomplishment above friends, family, recreation, exercise, and more. In some cases, they feel uncomfortable if they do not have something work related to do (Forbes, 1979).

SELF-ADMINISTERED QUIZZES

Since system-sponsored programs in stress awareness and management for educators have been few in number, the individual teacher or administrator must assume responsibility for learning the symptoms and then applying the appropriate stress-management technique. The self-administered quizzes provided in the previous chapter and in other locations in this text will provide some assistance in identifying symptoms and risk factors. The remainder of this chapter provides insight into the most common symptoms and how to recognize them.

People often recognize or are willing to accept the existence of symptoms of illness only when they reach the point of causing pain or significantly interfering with daily functioning. They are not attuned to their bodies or ignore basic warning signs even though they are aware of them. Some people will wait months or years before giving proper attention to the symptoms of a disorder (Girdano & Everly, 1979). The same holds true in recognizing and responding to the symptoms of stress.

RECOGNIZING GOOD HEALTH

For most people, identifying symptoms of stress, illness, and disorders is not difficult. They simply know that they are not experiencing good health. Aches, pains, and feelings of discomfort indicate that something has gone wrong. Good health is defined as the absence of illness. Therefore, identifying symptoms of illness requires an understanding of good health.

The "Wellness" Concept

People measure mental health and well-being in different ways. They rarely measure mental health as the simple absence of mental illness. In fact, many people do not acknowledge mental illness. Unlike physical illness, the signs of mental disorder are vague. The average person lacks the skills to make precise diagnoses about his or her mental health. The traditional view is that a mentally healthy person is a well-adjusted person. When some people feel excessive mental strain, anxiety, conflict, anger, or grief, they may acknowledge the need for some assistance to obtain relief. Others may deny the symptoms because of the stereotyped image of mentally ill people.

Jahoda (1979) offers certain traits and dimensions of behavior to guide a person in recognizing good mental health. He states that a mentally healthy person has:

—A realistic understanding of himself
—The ability to become mature and to learn by experience
—An integrated personality
—Sufficient independence to enable himself to make decisions and act on them
—A realistic perception of his social environment
—The ability to control himself and, to some extent, his environment

Understanding the traits that characterize sound physical and mental health can assist a person in identifying the symptoms of stress. Many stress symptoms are obvious while others are subtle and require monitoring over an extended period of time. Some stress symptoms can only be identified through a consultation with a physician, dentist, counselor, or other professional.

Seeking professional assistance is one of the best methods for identifying the symptoms of stress. Only a dentist, for example, can identify signs of tooth grinding, which is acknowledged to be one of the most common stress symptoms. Most tooth grinding occurs during periods of sleep and goes unrecognized by the individual. Current dental research acknowledges tooth grinding as a high predictor of stress (Kinzer, 1979).

WARNING SIGNS OF STRESS

As stated earlier, the symptoms of stress may be recognized with some ease. In considering the following warning signs, it should be remembered that each person is unique and that the causes and manifestation of stress will be equally unique. One person may experience severe headaches and constant indigestion. Another may experience lower back pain and fatigue. Both people may be responding to similar causes of stress at home and on the job.

Selye (1976) has identified the primary warning signs exhibited by people under stress. The following list represents his findings as well as those of other leading professionals who have worked in the field of stress awareness and management.

—General irritability, hyperexcitation, or depression
—Dryness of the throat and mouth
—Impulsive behavior
—Emotional instability
—Inability to concentrate, general disorientation
—Feelings of weakness
—Dizziness
—Loss of reality
—Fatigue
—Floating anxiety or irrational fears
—Emotional tension, a sense of being "keyed up"
—Trembling
—Nervous tics or excessive nervous habits
—Tendency to be easily startled
—Nervous, high-pitched laughter

—Frequent urination
—Diarrhea
—Indigestion, stomach ailments, vomiting
—Migraine headaches, frequent headaches
—Premenstrual tension
—Abnormal menstrual cycles
—Lower back pain
—Neck pain
—Chest pain
—Loss of appetite
—Compulsive eating
—Excessive smoking, increased smoking
—Increased use of prescribed drugs
—Alcohol dependency
—Drug addiction
—Nightmares

—Stuttering or other speech difficulties
—Tooth grinding
—Insomnia, not being able to sleep
—Sweating
—Neurotic behavior
—Psychoses
—Accident-prone behavior (Greenberg & Valletutti, 1980; Yates, 1979)

Tressider (1977) divided warning signs into two categories, physical symptoms and mental symptoms. This division is an effective way to categorize the typical symptoms of stress.

Physical Symptoms

—Excess weight, with consideration of height and weight
—High blood pressure
—Lack of appetite
—Impulsive eating
—Frequent heartburn
—Chronic diarrhea
—Chronic constipation
—Loss of sleep
—Constant fatigue
—The need for daily medication such as aspirin
—Frequent headaches
—Muscle spasms
—Sense of "fullness" without having eaten
—Shortness of breath
—Tendency toward fainting
—Tendency toward nausea
—Tendency toward sudden outbursts of tears
—Inability to cry
—Sexual disorders such as frigidity or impotence
—Excessive nervous energy

Mental Signs

—Constant feelings of uneasiness
—Irritability toward family
—Irritability toward associates at work
—General sense of boredom
—Recurring feelings of hopelessness in coping with life
—Anxiety about money
—Irrational fear of disease
—Fear of death
—Feelings of suppressed anger
—Inability to laugh easily and openly
—Feelings of rejection by family members
—Feelings of despair at failing as a parent
—Feelings of dread toward an approaching weekend
—Reluctance to vacation
—Sense that problems cannot be discussed with others
—Inability to concentrate
—Inability to complete one task before beginning another
—Fear of heights, enclosed places, thunderstorms, earthquakes, etc.

Psychosocial Signs

The symptoms of stress may also be psychosocial. They may be exhibited in interaction with others at work, home, and during social events. These symptoms are rarely associated with specific physical diseases and disorders. Psychosocial symptoms of stress include:

—Increased use of alcohol	—Slamming objects
—Increased use of drugs	—Changes in posture
—Increased use of tobacco	—Hyperventilation
—Weight gain	—Increased spending of money
—Weight loss	—Reckless behavior
—Increased activity	—Poor judgment
—Reduced activity	—Increased sexual activity
—Pacing the floor	—Reduced sexual activity
—Wringing hands	—Loss of effectiveness at work
—Worried look	—Increased eating
—Throwing objects	—Reduced eating (Aronson & Mas-
—Kicking objects	cia, 1981)

STRESS SYMPTOMS AND EDUCATORS

The symptoms listed above apply to all people, regardless of their occupation. The physical symptoms are as applicable to people in education professions as they are to those in medicine or social work.

Statistically, the number of medical insurance claims being made by teachers is greater than the number of claims made by people in most other professions. One recent study has shown that the life expectancy for teachers is 4 years lower than the national average.

In England, studies have shown that deaths among male teachers who are approaching retirement have doubled during the past decade. Other studies have shown that the number of teachers qualifying for pensions due to mental or emotional breakdowns has tripled in recent years. A rapidly increasing number of studies are underway to document and measure the physical, mental, and emotional illnesses common to the education profession (Truch, 1980).

Hendrickson (1979) referred to teacher burnout as physical, attitudinal, and emotional exhaustion. The symptoms offered for teacher burnout closely parallel those of stress. In fact, many people believe that stress and burnout are synonymous. Others state that stress on the job is a cause of burnout, burnout being the end result. In any case, the relationship between stress and burnout is significant.

Educators suffering from burnout may feel tired, depressed, and physically run down. They may experience sleeplessness on a regular basis. Frequently, they may also suffer from minor maladies such as colds, headaches, diarrhea, and dizziness. In time, if these ailments are not addressed and changes do not occur, they may grow into more serious problems such as ulcers, colitis, asthma, or sexual difficulties.

If the ailments continue, the burnout cycle begins. Educators grow depressed and disappointed by their own physical ills. They find it uncomfortable to play with their students during recreation or lunch periods. They have difficulty lecturing and being enthused about their lessons when they're feeling dizzy or suffer from severe headaches. Then they feel guilty because of their self-judged inadequacies. Their self-concept and self-esteem are lowered and they begin to question the value of remaining in the field of education.

The ailments of the body soon cause ailments of the mind. They then transfer to perceived ailments within the educational system. Eventually, they may develop into feelings of inadequacy as a person. At this point, personal relationships suffer. If unchecked, burnout can ultimately lead to a total emotional breakdown (Hendrickson & LaBarca, 1979).

Additional information on burnout in education and its relationship to stress is provided in Chapters 5 and 10 of this text.

Warning Signs for the Educator

There are 15 basic warning signs of stress. Each of these may be seen on the job, at home, or in social interactions. The following list offers the basic warning signs.

1. Abrupt change in typical behavior pattern
2. Rapid mood change
3. Overly suspicious
4. Excessive use of alcohol
5. Overhostility
6. Extreme defensiveness
7. Frequent illness
8. Excessive nervous habits
9. Accident prone
10. Taking unnecessary chances
11. Becoming obsessive about working
12. Sleep disturbances
13. Decrease in work performance
14. Depression
15. Use of excessive violence

SUMMARY

One of the worst things a person can do is become paranoid about stress and its symptoms and warning signs. Response to stress should be the same as for any other illness or disorder. When symptoms appear, the best response is an early one. Taking steps to reduce and manage stress before it becomes severe is as effective as taking steps to avoid a serious cold by responding to its early symptoms.

When an educator identifies that she or he has several of the symptoms, appropriate action should be taken. The latter part of this text provides a wide variety of techniques for effectively reducing, eliminating, or living with stress. Particular attention is given to managing stress in education.

The symptoms and warning signs are cautionary signs that potential danger exists. This implies that the potential also exists for the danger to be eliminated or controlled. It does not imply that it is too late to take corrective measures. Almost every person has the ability to respond effectively and favorably to stress. In using the warning signs offered in this chapter, it is important to avoid the tendency to label other people's behavior as stress prone. This may result in a person's overlooking his or her own behaviors and symptoms.

REFERENCES

Aronson, & Mascia. *The Stress management workbook: An action plan for taking control of your life and health.* Appleton Consumer Health Guides, 1981.

Forbes, R. *Life stress.* New York: Doubleday & Co., 1979.

Girdano, D., & Everly, G. *Controlling stress and tension.* Englewood Cliffs, NJ: Prentice-Hall, 1979.

Greenberg, S. F., & Valletutti, P. J. *Stress and the helping professions.* Baltimore: Paul H. Brookes Publishing Co., 1980.

Hendrickson, J. M., & La Barca, A. *Spice of life.* New York: Harcourt Brace Jovanovich, 1979.

Jahoda, M. In: G. N. Grob (ed.), *Current concepts in positive mental health.* New York: Arno Press, 1979.

Kinzer, N. S. *Stress and the American woman.* New York: Anchor Press/Doubleday, 1979.

Selye, H. *Stress in health and disease.* Woburn, MA: Butterworth Publishers, 1976.

Tressider, J. *Feel younger, live longer.* Skokie, IL: Rand McNally & Co., 1977.

Truch, S. *Teacher burnout: And what to do about it.* Novato, CA: Academic Therapy Publications, 1980.

Yates, J. *Managing stress.* New York: American Management Association, 1979.

Chapter 10

Preparing to Manage Stress

Stress has an impact on every aspect of a person's daily activity. It can affect a person environmentally (through such things as weather, living conditions, and public services) and socially. Its impact may be mental as well as physical. It influences a person's perceptions, thoughts, and anticipations. It involves a person's actions and inactions. Because stress affects almost every aspect of a person's daily life, there are no mystical, quick cures for controlling or reducing it (Girdano & Everly, 1979).

PERSONAL COMMITMENT

Stress management is not necessarily difficult. Just like any other self-improvement effort, managing stress requires personal commitment. The educator who wants to cope more effectively with the strains and anxieties of the school day will have to take initiative to find the techniques best suited to his or her life-style and then make the commitment to improving it. Stress management requires:

1. Commitment
2. Initiative
3. Willpower
4. Knowledge
5. Common sense

At first glance, this list may seem frightening. Many people may feel doomed to failure because they have had misfortune with previous efforts to diet or organize themselves or complete unfinished projects. While stress management involves the same basic principles required to do well at other endeavors, it does not have to be difficult. Many stress-management techniques are quite simple and can be implemented by anyone. The foundation for a successful stress-management program is the willingness of the educator to assume responsibility for his or her own well-being.

PROFESSIONAL GUIDANCE

In preparing to implement a stress-management program, many people seek professional guidance. They make inquiries of their family physician, dentist, counselor, or clergyman. They seek suggestions on the best possible techniques to use. They also receive encouragement from people whose professional opinions they respect.

Not every person who wants to pursue stress management should or does contact others for input. They are satisfied with learning all that they can on their own and choosing the techniques they deem appropriate to their particular needs. In fact, many people are embarrassed to admit that they are reacting to stress negatively. They judge that reacting to stress negatively and wanting to relieve some of the strains and anxieties of their life are signs of weakness or failure. In today's society, fortunately, this stigma is disappearing as business, industry, government, and individuals are becoming more aware of the impact of stress on daily functioning.

While seeking professional guidance is not essential to beginning a stress-management program, input from a physician should definitely be sought before engaging in such activities as dieting and participating in physical exercise, both of which may aid in reducing stress. Such input is vital to avoid complications, such as injury or illness, which may ultimately compound the person's daily stress. This is common sense . . . an essential element in stress management.

RECOGNIZING INDIVIDUALITY

Every person is an individual, with his or her very own strengths and weaknesses, happiness and sorrow, joys and frustrations. In education, a large group may form the organization (elementary teachers, specialists, principals, professors, etc.), but unique individuals exist under the label. As such, no two people will react to stress in exactly the same way. And, no two people will manage the stress in their lives exactly the same way (Morse & Furst, 1979).

In getting ready to implement a self-help program, people have a natural tendency to look toward their friends and neighbors to see what they have done and how various programs have worked. This is commendable when the information is sought as a means of gaining knowledge. It is dangerous, though, when someone else's program is adopted blindly without regard to personal differences.

One key to success in stress management is finding the best program or techniques available. Once information, like that offered in the following chapters, is obtained, a personal stress-management plan should be developed. It should focus on techniques to reduce stress on both a short-term and long-term basis. It should be practical and designed so that it fits comfortably into the educator's daily activities. If the plan is not designed to accommodate personal needs or provide some immediate as well as long-term relief, the program may not be effective.

Since stress comes to educators in all varieties, their emotional and psychological strength will be significant in determining resistance. Some people break down in the face of adversity while others take it well and are even spurred to heights of achievement by it. Therefore, to say that stress causes psychological or physical illnesses such as depression and tension is to show only one side of a coin. Depression and tension may be caused by stress and may also be a source of stress to people. For others, depression and tension may be catalysts to stress reduction and greater achievement. Response to stress is unique to the individual.

THREE WAYS TO MANAGE STRESS

There are three general ways in which people manage stress. They may: 1) cope with the stress as it exists, 2) fight against it, or 3) flee from it. In developing a stress-management plan, a person will have to decide which approach is best suited to dealing with specific stressors in his or her life.

Coping with stress as it exists and fighting against it are techniques that closely parallel the body's effort to maintain physical equilibrium. This is seen in how the body reacts to an aggressor such as a disease-causing organism. The human body will have syntoxic reactions, in which there is a state of passive tolerance between bodily systems and an aggressor. The body will also have catatoxic reactions in which chemical changes occur to create enzymes that attack and attempt to destroy an aggressor. An individual has the same basic approaches available for dealing with stress as the body does for dealing with disease-causing agents (Yates, 1979).

Fleeing from the source of stress is not an option available within the body as a response to an aggressor. Yet, this is a viable approach to reducing stress in a person's life. For example, a person walking down a dimly lit street may see a group of tough-looking men hanging out on the corner up ahead obviously looking to cause trouble. The person's options for dealing with this stress are to continue walking, passively accepting their presence and any attack that may occur. This is somewhat like the body's syntoxic approach. The person may proceed along the street and fight the thugs when an attack occurs. This parallels the catatoxic approach of the body. Finally, the person may turn and walk in another direction, thereby fleeing from and eliminating the source of stress.

The individual walking down the street will most likely choose one of the three options cited. To stand still and accept the stress would be a useless endeavor. The stress would continue and might possibly grow as the group on the corner began walking in the person's direction.

The choice of technique for dealing with the stress of the street thugs is based on the person's commitment, initiative, willpower, knowledge, and common sense. In more practical day-to-day situations, both professional and personal, it is important for a person to carefully choose the technique for managing stress that provides the best possible results for the situation at hand.

Should a person passively accept stress, aggressively attack the stressor, or flee from it? The wrong choice could easily backfire. For example, a teacher who identifies a particular parent as a major source of stress will suffer professionally if he or she totally ignores that parent (fleeing) or punches the parent in the nose (attacking). The easiest technique for dealing with the stress may be to ignore the parent. The most desirable technique may be to punch the parent in the nose. However, the best technique, based on common sense and the teacher's knowledge of the system, may be to accept the parent. This may not be easy, but the alternatives will create far more stress than they will resolve. The point is that choosing the best technique for managing stress requires some planning. It also shows that the best technique for managing stress may not necessarily be the easiest or most desirable.

HOLISTIC APPROACH

Rather than seeing the person as a complete whole, western philosophers believe that three aspects of body, mind, and spirit make up the person. Unlike other countries of the world that view a person as an integrated whole, western nations have focused on separate parts. For example, the healing profession has established separate fields to deal with various areas. Physicians heal the body, psychiatrists and psychologists treat the mind. The clergy attend to the soul (Goldberg, 1978).

In recent years, westerners have begun to adopt the holistic approach. They've begun to view human beings as single entities, focusing on the interaction between their psychological, biological, social, and environmental functions. One reason for the shift in traditional thinking has been the recent research on eastern concepts using the scientific techniques of the western world. It has been shown that many eastern concepts, which are holistic, work well.

> The holistic approach views the body processes as not being completely involuntary. It holds that the individual should play an active role both in maintaining good health and in treating ill health. It indicates that the ill can no longer be seen as innocent victims of their bodies, completely absolved from any responsibility for the illness (Girdano & Everly, 1979).

The holistic approach can be applied to stress management in that stress affects people physically, mentally, and emotionally. Stress can be increased or reduced by how people think, interact with others, treat themselves physically, develop and apply life goals and values, and interact with their environment. Therefore, efforts to control stress must focus on the whole person. The best approach to stress management is a holistic one. It focuses on the whole person. Girdano and Everly (1979) related holism to stress management by defining it as the concept underlying an approach to controlling stress that deals with the complete life-style of the individual, incorporating intervention at several levels—physical, psychological, and social—simultaneously.

> Our habits, our priorities, and our life styles have all been called into question. Newer, healthier ways of living are being advocated by health experts. . . . First we must have a clear understanding of stress so that we may hope to tame it. To do this, we must define it, learn to recognize its effects, minimize these effects, and, most importantly, strive holistically to prevent them through an informed program of coordinated health practices tailored to our own individual needs (Goldberg, 1978).

ESTABLISHING A SUPPORT SYSTEM AND CALLING ON PERSONAL RESOURCES

In her text, *Stress and the American Woman,* Norma Scott Kinzer made two key statements that should serve as foundation principles for every educator who wants to reduce the negative effects of stress. First, "there ain't no free lunch." Second, "if you don't like it, change it." Her statements point out that any stress-management program will require some effort, energy, and commitment. While some stress-management techniques are simple and easy to implement, short-range and long-range stress-reduction programs will require work. In addition, she points out that people are, in fact, in control of their own lives. Every educator is in control of his or her own destiny as it relates to stress (Kinzer, 1979).

If a teacher wanted to put on a holiday program for a school, he or she would first seek out and establish a support team. This team might include administrators, other teachers, students, parent volunteers, and custodians. He or she would also evaluate personal talents to determine how much could be accomplished without the aid of others. No steps would be taken to conduct rehearsals until support systems and personal resources have been assessed. Similarly, personal resources and support systems must be assessed and gathered before beginning a stress-management program.

Calling on the Body's Own Resources

Most people have a bountiful supply of internal resources from which to draw. The resources of the body and mind are amazing. Calling on these resources is essential as a first step in preparing to manage stress. "Since the environment is unlikely to grow less complex or more stable, we must find within our own bodies a physiologic means of dealing with the demands of twentieth-century life'' (Benson, 1975). The value of a person's own physical resources in reducing stress, particularly as they relate to a structured program of physical activity, are unparalleled. Their benefits in preventing the negative effects of stress are such that if they could be bottled and sold for people to take in daily doses, the bottling and sales agents would grow wealthy beyond compare (Girdano & Everly, 1979). Dale Carnegie, whose guidance has helped people to stop worrying, cites that many of the physical weaknesses and lack of physical strengths of people are simply habit-based. He notes that tension and stress are merely the result of bad habits and, conversely, relaxation and stress reduction are products of good habits. And, good habits are within everyone's reach (Carnegie, 1974).

Resources of the Mind

Just as a person can call upon physical resources to reduce stress, he or she can also call upon the resources of the mind. Mental attitude alone can make a difference in how a person reacts to stressors (Culligan & Sedlacek, 1976). Strong psychological adjustment has been shown to effectively offset the dysfunctional effects of stress. For example, one of the main factors in determining reaction to stress is the cognitive process of perception. How a person thinks about or perceives a certain stressor is important to the effect it will have. Managing thoughts, feelings, and perceptions can be effective in minimizing stress (Yates, 1979).

Family and Friends

In addition to drawing on one's own physical and mental strengths, an educator should consider family and friends as components of a stress-management support system. Coping with stress is easier when people feel that others are available to offer encouragement. When family and friends provide support, people generally find it easier to deal with the turmoil of disappointments, conflicts, anxieties, and depressions.

Developing a personal and reasonably satisfying support system is one of the most important and effective methods for coping with stress. Having people, whether they be fellow educators, family members, or friends, to help share concerns and problems, helps to keep things in perspective and make them more manageable. Feelings of being out of control or defeated are minimized (Kinzer, 1979).

Calling on a person's family, friends, and inner resources may sound simplistic. In fact, if family and friends or physical health are sources of stress, using them as stress-management resources will be difficult. Most people, though, have the ability to call upon their physical and mental energy to tackle stress. Most people also have intimate friends and co-workers with whom they are close. These people provide excellent support.

The Power of Positive Thinking

Using inner reserves of mental and physical energy involves the power of positive thinking. It requires that the educator make a commitment to stress management. It requires that an enthusiastic, positive approach be taken. Stress can be managed. The tensions, anxieties, frustrations, and physical ailments that an educator experiences can be reduced.

In part, successful stress management is a self-fulfilled prophecy. A person expects something to happen and then acts in ways that will increase the likelihood that the expectation will be met. If someone who is ill expects to get well, he or she will be more likely to take medication and follow the physician's prescribed plan. The chances for recovery are increased. Conversely, if he or she feels that the illness will linger for a long period no matter what the doctor says, the physician's guidance may not be followed and the illness will linger. The basic characteristic of a self-fulfilled prophecy is the "reinforcing cycle." This is when an expectation of success often leads to success, which in turn provides evidence that the original expectation was correct and good. A negative expectation results in an unsuccessful outcome which, in turn, validates the negative expectation. The expectation, positive or negative, grows stronger the more the cycle is repeated (Simonton, 1978).

Even the most stressed of educators should be optimistic about reducing the causes of tension, anxiety, and frustration in their lives. A positive attitude toward stress reduction is second only to recognizing that stress exists and is taking its toll. It cannot be understated that a positive attitude is the foundation for making changes necessary for mental, physical, and emotional well-being. Carnegie emphasizes the importance of positive attitude as a means for people to shape their own ends. He notes that a positive attitude toward addressing a problem or concern will result in a rapid change for the better. By refusing to adopt a positive attitude, a person's efforts toward problem-solving will remain weak (Carnegie, 1974).

DEVELOPING A PLAN

Developing a stress-management plan can be as simple or complex as a person desires. But, it should never be *more* complex than a person desires. The following chapters provide a variety of stress-management techniques. Which ones and how many a person chooses to implement are matters of personal preference. The extent of a stress-management plan and the number of items in it are not as important as making a firm commitment to do something.

An educator should take some time to think about his or her plan. The following questions should be considered:

1. In what aspects of my life do I need to reduce stress most?

2. What techniques for reducing stress seem best suited to my life-style and my likes and dislikes?
3. How can I rely on my family for support?
4. How can I rely on my friends and co-workers for support?
5. How much time do I have to commit to stress-reduction activities each day?
6. Have I developed a positive attitude toward wanting to reduce stress? If not, what must I do to become more optimistic?
7. What books and materials should I review before I start?
8. What stresses and strains do I want to reduce immediately? Which ones will I have to address over a long period of time?
9. What does my physician say about beginning a stress-management program?

The First Steps

The first step in any stress-management plan should be a visit to a physician. There is no substitute for this. No matter how much or how little a person will undertake, a checkup should be included. A family physician will be familiar with a person's family and medical history. This information is invaluable. There are other reasons for getting a physical examination prior to starting a stress-management program. First, a checkup may identify stress-related problems not previously recognized. Second, the physician may show that certain stress-reduction techniques may be more harmful than beneficial. He or she will place limitations on the techniques to be used. And, the physician may suggest additional and better ways to reduce stress.

The second step in an educator's effort to reduce stress should be a review of some of the material available on the subject. This text provides a myriad of techniques and suggestions. Many of them are discussed in brief in an effort to give the teacher or administrator a comprehensive overview. Some techniques and suggestions are also presented in detail. However, just as most teachers would not prepare a lesson plan based solely on one reference source, they should not prepare a stress-management plan without considering available literature and research. Hundreds of books and thousands of articles have been published on the topic of stress. With this wealth of knowledge available, an educator can pick and choose until the best suited techniques are found.

SUMMARY

Stress management is not necessarily difficult. Like any other personal improvement effort, it requires some planning. With a personal plan, an educator will be more likely to succeed in reducing and controlling stress.

Stress management requires commitment, initiative, willpower, knowledge, and common sense. Professional guidance should be sought prior to the start of any plan. This may include a visit to a physician, psychologist, psychiatrist, counselor, or clergymember.

Every person is an individual with his or her unique personality, physical makeup and other characteristics. As such, no single stress-management plan will be right for every person. Information obtained from friends, books, and other sources provides valuable sources of knowledge from which a personal plan may be developed. As unique individuals, people manage stress in three ways. They cope with it as it exists, fight against it, or flee from it. All are acceptable coping techniques. A stress-management plan will involve one, two, or all three of these coping methods. The choice of technique will be based on the individual's needs, commitment, and personal makeup.

The holistic approach to stress management considers a person's psychological, biological, social, and environmental functioning. It considers the whole person. Traditionally, the western world, and particularly the health professions, have considered humans to be made up of separate entities. In planning a stress-management program, an educator should take a holistic approach because stress in one aspect of a person's life will generally have an impact on the other aspects.

A good support system will prove invaluable in a stress-management program. Such a system will include the support of family, friends, and co-workers. They can be a key to success in stress management, offering encouragement and reinforcement. In addition to calling upon others, an educator must call upon his or her inner resources. The resources of the mind and body are plentiful. One such resource is attitude and positive thinking. A person's success in stress reduction will be contingent, in part, on a positive attitude. There is validity in self-fulfilled prophecy. Therefore, expectation of difficulty and failure will breed difficulty and failure. A positive, optimistic attitude toward stress reduction, a self-fulfilled prophecy of success, will breed success and a life of reduced and controlled stress.

As most educators are aware, any successful program, whether it be a classroom lesson, a play, or an athletic competition, requires planning. It requires reviewing available data, involving others, and outlining attainable steps. A stress-management program is no different. It requires planning. It must be designed to suit the educator's individual needs and should address both short-range and long-term stress reduction. The first steps of the plan should include a visit to a physician, who will provide invaluable suggestions, and a review of information. With this type of preparation, the educator who seeks to reduce and control stress in his or her life will be on the road to success.

REFERENCES

Benson, H. *The relaxation response.* New York: William Morrow and Co., 1975.

Carnegie, D. *How to stop worrying and start living.* New York: Pocket Books, 1974.

Culligan, M., & Sedlacek, K. *How to kill stress before it kills you.* New York: Grosset & Dunlap, 1976.

Girdano, D., & Everly, G. *Controlling stress and tension*. Englewood Cliffs, NJ: Prentice-Hall, 1979.

Goldberg, P. *Executive health*. New York: McGraw-Hill Book Co., 1978.

Kinzer, N. *Stress and the American woman*. New York: Anchor Press/Doubleday, 1979.

Morse, D. R., & Furst, M. L. *Stress for success: A holistic approach to stress and its management*. New York: Van Nostrand Reinhold Co., 1979.

Simonton, C. *Getting well again*. Los Angeles: J. P. Tarcher, Inc., 1978.

Yates, J. *Managing stress*. New York: American Management Association, 1979.

Chapter 11

Diet and Nutrition

H ow and what a person eats may either compound or reduce the negative effects of stress. Certain foods and eating habits may induce stress-like reactions in people and compound ailments that already exist. However, developing eating habits that reduce the negative effects of stress is not too difficult. Sticking to a nutritional diet and sound eating habits is one of the two best defenses against disease. The other is regular exercise (Culligan & Sedlacek, 1976). This chapter focuses on diet and eating habits. Exercise is addressed in the next chapter.

Poor dietary habits affect all people negatively. In education, where the stresses, strains, and responsibilities abound, a poor diet may be the teacher's or administrator's worst enemy. A poor diet may lead to ill health or excess weight that may, in turn, cause stress. A poor diet may also be the result of the job, particularly when time is not allotted to eat properly during the workday. Poor diet may not only be a cause of stress but also the result of stress.

In 1977, the United States Senate Select Committee on Nutrition and Human Needs conducted a study on dietary changes that have occurred during the past several decades. One such change identified by the Committee was a decrease in the consumption of apples by 70%. Another was the increase in the consumption of food dyes by 995%. The Committee's report made some practical recommendations for change in the American diet:

1. Consumption of fruits, vegetables, and whole grains should be increased.
2. Adults should substitute lowfat and nonfat milk for whole milk, and lowfat dairy products for those with high fat content.
3. Foods high in total fat or saturated fats should be decreased and replaced with those with polyunsaturated fats.
4. Consumption of animal fats should be reduced.
5. Consumption of butter fat, eggs, and other high cholesterol sources should be reduced.

6. Consumption of refined and other processed sugars should be reduced, as well as foods high in refined sugar content.
7. Consumption of salt and foods high in salt content should be reduced (Matteson & Ivancevich, 1982).

Effective stress resistance is contingent, in part, on personal nutrition. The old saying "you are what you eat" is based on more truth than most people believe. Maintaining energy reserves to ward off stress and illness requires a well-balanced diet.

An elementary school teacher observed over the years that students always seemed tense and hyperactive in the afternoons. She worked hard to overcome this phenomenon by putting extra effort into motivating the students. She saved her best lessons for the afternoon. But her efforts failed and she grew increasingly anxious over the students' afternoon personalities. In seeking to identify causes, she never considered food. Yet, the students' lunches were filled with salts, refined sugars, and food additives. These foods not only fill the body with empty calories, but also drain valuable nutrients from the system. She was attempting to overcome physical reactions in the students with dynamic lesson plans. She was doomed to some degree of failure.

In cultures where the average life span is high (ages 80–90), total intake of calories by adults averages 1500–1800 per day. In studies with rats, controlled fasts resulted in increased life spans by as much as 50%. Insurance company actuarial charts show that life expectancy is longer for lightweight people (Shaffer, 1982).

OBESITY

The most common stress disease related to dietary habits is obesity. Often thought of as a physical condition, obesity is harmful. It creates physical and emotional difficulties.

> An obese person is, by the stern standards of our society, unattractive, and this simple fact hampers not only his relations with other people, but also his feelings about himself. In addition, the extra poundage places him under a continuous physical strain. Every time he climbs the stairs or runs for a bus it is as if he were carrying a sack of books with him—all his physical equipment has to work harder to move the load. As a result, obesity in an individual is often eventually joined by other ailments—kidney disease, diabetes, high blood pressure, gall bladder problems, or heart trouble. No direct causative link has yet been established between cardiovascular disease and obesity, but most nutritionists assume that it exists, simply because the two go together so often (McQuade & Aikman, 1974).

EDUCATORS' EATING HABITS

Educators tend to do two things very well regarding their diet, both of which are harmful. They eat fast food and they eat food fast. In a faculty lunch room, it is commonplace to find lunchmeat sandwiches, bits and pieces from the school's cafeteria line, coffee, tea, cola, potato chips, and an odd assortment of pies and cakes. All of these items are consumed in haste so that the teachers and administrators can return to tasks ranging from cafeteria duty to preparing for the afternoon class.

Immoderate consumption of coffee, tea, cola, chocolate, sugar, or flour products can make an educator anxious, irritable, tired, unmotivated, and, over a period of time, physically ill, suffering from such disorders as heart attack and high blood pressure. For example, a 6-ounce cup of coffee contains 108 milligrams of caffeine. A cup of tea contains 90 milligrams. At 250 milligrams of caffeine, the body begins to experience adverse effects in the form of stress reaction symptoms. One text states that 20 cups at one time is considered a lethal dose. Caffeine, which is also present in cola (50–60 milligrams) and chocolate (20 milligrams in a 1-ounce bar), stimulates the release of stress-producing hormones. It results in an initial burst of energy but then drains the system by causing lowered blood sugar. This then causes feelings of drowsiness or headaches and increases the desire for more caffeine. The cycle is repeated when the second dose of caffeine is consumed, creating stress factors beyond those usually associated with the classroom or educational administration.

Caffeine is not the only culprit in the educator's diet. Nutritionally, most educators (in fact, most Americans) leave much to be desired. In a recent year, the average American consumed 370 12-ounce bottles of soda; 36.8 pounds of frozen potatoes, mostly in the form of fast food french fries; 12 fast food hamburgers, 11 pieces of fast food fried chicken, 76,650 calories worth of alcoholic beverages, and 102 pounds of refined sugar (Matteson & Ivancevich, 1982).

THE FOOD GROUPS

Early in most people's education, a teacher stood before the class pointing to charts of fruits, vegetables, breads, meats, milk, and other nutritious items. The teacher talked about the importance of the food groups and recommended the number of servings of each group that should be eaten every day. That same teacher probably failed to eat breakfast, and gobbled a sandwich and cup of coffee for lunch.

There are four food groups: the milk group, meat group, vegetable group, and cereal or grain group. Yates (1979) noted that when he asked a group of 25 professional people to name the groups, not one person responded correctly. In a seminar on stress management, a group of 40 high school teachers were asked the same question. About one-third of the teachers knew the answer. When asked how many portions of each group the average adult should consume, not one teacher responded correctly.

There is no substitute for a balanced diet, one that includes some or all of the foods essential to the health and maintenance of the body. The fundamental rule for sound nutrition is to eat good food, maintain a balanced diet, and keep weight within normal limits.

THE IMPACT OF DIET

There are almost as many books on nutrition and the effects of food on the body and mind as there are on how to diet. The relationship between the foods people eat and their mental, physical, and emotional state is a concrete one. People who skip meals or do not eat a balanced diet most likely find themselves tiring easily, having shorter attention spans, and forgetting things more quickly. On days when a person has difficulty concentrating, he or she need only think back to breakfast to find a possible cause. Was breakfast a doughnut and cup of coffee instead of a bowl of whole grain cereal? The root of forgetfulness and lack of concentration may lie in nutrition.

Many years of Iowa Breakfast Studies showed that school students who skipped or skimped on breakfast found it very difficult to remain alert until lunchtime. The researchers showed that a sound, balanced diet not only kept the students alert enough to learn for an extended period, but also helped them to remember what they studied. A nutritious breakfast proved to be a stimulant to the students' memories.

In memory experiments at the National Institute of Mental Health, people were given large doses of choline before memorizing lists of words. Choline is a natural substance found in such foods as eggs, soybeans, and liver, that helps produce acetylcholine, a chemical that transmits nerve impulses in the brain and is responsible for functions such as memory. When given the choline, the people were able to recall the lists far better than when they attempted to learn without the substance (Winter, 1976).

THINGS TO DO

Maintaining proper nutrition is not difficult or expensive. It does not require that educators change their life-style to a diet of bean curd and alfalfa sprouts. It does not require the willpower of an athlete training for the Olympics. Nor does it require that people give up their favorite foods. It does require some initiative and commitment.

The remainder of this chapter provides a variety of techniques for maintaining proper weight and a nutritious diet. It also provides recommendations on substances to avoid, such as certain food additives. The keys to success in maintaining a sound nutritional program are **moderation** and **common sense.**

They are far more effective and far less expensive than any diet pills or vitamin supplements on the market.

Eat a Variety of Foods

Eating a variety of foods provides a strong foundation for obtaining most of the nutrients that the body needs. Yet, most educators fall into eating ruts. They eat the same few foods repeatedly. They rarely branch out and experiment with new items in their diet. To avoid this, they should mix foods from the various groups and avoid the "rut" of eating the same foods for breakfast and lunch every day. Milk or juice with lunch 1 or 2 days a week could be substituted for a soft drink, coffee, or tea. And, a lunch from home can be packed instead of buying prepared foods from the school cafeteria or a fast food restaurant every day. Educators should consider some or all of the following tips:

1. When planning meals, choose from the basic food groups (milk, meat, fruits and vegetables, and grains). Almost all people learned about the various food groups from their elementary school teacher, but few realized how sound and important this information is to good health.
2. Eat more fresh fruit and green, leafy vegetables. Most cafeterias will provide salad plates for educators if requested to do so.
3. Use whole grains instead of plain, white flour. Whole grains provide vitamins and are an excellent source of needed fiber.
4. Place emphasis on variety in the foods eaten, whether in the home, a school cafeteria, or a restaurant.
5. Maintain ideal weight. Almost all people feel better about themselves when they look fit. Proper weight maintenance is not only healthy but can improve a person's self-esteem.
6. Avoid too much fat, saturated fat, and cholesterol. Research continues to find evidence linking these food elements to poor health.
7. Eat adequate amounts of starch and fiber.
8. Avoid too much sugar, especially refined, white table sugar.
9. Avoid too much sodium or salt. It is considered a risk factor to poor health.

Each of the above items is easier said than done. Most people have heard or read them many times. Implementing them, though, is difficult. The following provides some easy-to-implement, low-cost guides to fostering proper nutritional habits. By selecting some or all of them, educators will find that they will feel better, look better, and maintain proper weight more effectively.

Eat More Fruits and Green Vegetables Buy a salad for lunch instead of the usual sandwich. Make fruit or fresh vegetables the main dish for lunch 1 or 2 days a week. Keep a small container of fresh vegetable pieces in a desk drawer for snacking. When shopping, buy some unusual fruits and vegetables, ones that are not found in the refrigerator every week.

Use Whole Grains Today's highly processed grains are void of most of the nutrients that exist in whole grains. They provide calories without nutrients. Buy different types of breads including whole wheat and rye to break the polished flour habit. When baking, substitute one-third to one-half whole wheat flour for the white flour in the recipe. Change breakfast cereals during the week, including some of the whole grain, natural ones on the market.

Maintain Ideal Weight The more an educator's weight exceeds the ideal, the greater the risk of poor health and physical ailments. If the educator must lose weight, he or she should consult a physician to determine a realistic weight goal. When weight climbs, he or she should simply cut back on foods eaten instead of eliminating foods completely from the daily diet. For example, drink one beer instead of two, or order a regular hamburger instead of a double-decker. Serving sizes can be reduced. Using smaller plates and forks can aid this. Chopsticks are excellent for helping a person eat less and more slowly. Taking a walk or engaging in some form of physical activity before eating also reduces appetite.

Avoid Too Much Fat and Cholesterol Saturated fats and cholesterol, along with smoking, physical inactivity, and reaction to stress, are contributing risk factors in heart disease. Cholesterol is also associated with arteriosclerosis. To keep fat and cholesterol intake under control reduce consumption of red meats. When purchased, select lean meats and lean hamburger instead of cuts with large amounts of fat. When cooking, trim fat from meat and drain meat drippings. Reduce the amount of margarine, lard, and other fats used in cooking or on bread and vegetables. Use lowfat milk and cut down on the consumption of other fats when large amounts of whole milk or cheese are being used. Reduce the amount of fats called for in recipes. This can be done without loss of flavor or appearance. Limit intake of fried foods, especially those served by restaurants and fast food stores. Reduce amounts of creamed foods and rich desserts. Use fewer salad dressings and gravies.

Eat More Starch and Fiber Most people believe that starches are not healthy. Starches are necessary and important and, in reality, most people eat too few healthy starches. Therefore, they should increase the amount of fresh fruits and vegetables eaten, as these are a source of fiber. Eat more potatoes, sweet potatoes, yams, corn, peas, beans, and other legumes, but avoid the fatty, caloric toppings many people put on them. These foods provide bulk and make a person feel like she or he has eaten a very full meal, but they do not contain harmful fats or excessive calories. Grain products such as brown rice, oatmeal, whole wheat cereals, and breads should also be increased in the diet.

Avoid Too Much Sugar Most sugar in an educator's diet comes from processed foods and drinks such as soda, candy, and cakes rather than from the home sugar bowl. Many educators are addicted to sugar. Those who give it up often experience withdrawal and regularly fight cravings. Eating sweets is one of the most difficult nutritional habits to break. To help curb the sugar habit, educators should avoid or cut back on very sweet foods, especially those sweetened with refined sugar. Reduce the amount of sugar used in recipes. Rely more on canned juices and water than on sodas and other soft drinks. Limit sugar intake in the form of prepared foods such as jellies, jams, syrups, and sweetened cereals. Refined sugars are the primary ingredient in many of these products. Alternate cakes, ice cream, and other sweets with fresh fruits and nuts for dessert. Avoid putting the sugar bowl on the table. Purchase one less sweet dessert or snack product when shopping each week.

Avoid Too Much Salt and Sodium Commercially prepared foods are often produced with extremely high salt content. Like sugar, use of salt is a nutritional habit that should be broken or modified. Salt and sodium (the primary component in salt and soda) have been linked to disorders such as heart disease. Therefore, measures should be taken to reduce their intake. For instance, read ingredients to avoid purchasing too many foods heavy in salt or sodium content. Use less salt in cooking. This is not only healthy, but it helps people to discover the natural taste of foods. Avoid placing the salt shaker on the table. Discover and use other items to replace salt, such as lemon, parsley, pepper, thyme, and other spices. Reduce use of commercially prepared condiments such as ketchup, barbecue sauce, relishes, pickles, gravy mixes, and canned soups. They are extremely high in salt and sodium content. Use more fresh and frozen vegetables since canned items are generally packed in salt brine. Limit salty snacks such as pretzels and potato chips.

VITAMINS

Almost every library is filled with volumes of recent research on the use of vitamins. Some texts espouse the use of vitamins to cure everything from the simplest disorder to serious disease. There are also texts that dispute the claims about vitamin therapy.

It is impossible to provide a few general statements to guide educators in the proper use of vitamins. Individual needs are affected by many variables. For example, smokers have 30%–50% less vitamin C in their blood than non-smokers. People who drink alcoholic beverages have higher B-complex needs than nondrinkers.

Generally, scientific judgment about vitamins remains inconclusive. The following guidelines are offered by Matteson and Ivancevich (1982) regarding use of vitamins.

1. Eat well-balanced meals, giving considerable attention to fresh foods, particularly vegetables.
2. Take an all-purpose multivitamin supplement. This will cause no harm and may provide needed nutritional support.
3. During periods of stress or when experiencing any type of infection, increase intake of vitamin C. While the data on vitamin C are inconclusive, there are indications that it is effective, particularly in combating the effects of stress.

4. Regularly review articles and texts detailing the use of vitamins and vitamin therapy. New data are being obtained rapidly, and this week's information on vitamins may be outdated next week.

In addition to these four suggestions, educators should consult with their family physician. Many physicians have become knowledgeable about the uses and abuses of vitamins. Based on medical history, physicians may prescribe a specific vitamin program.

Self-prescribed vitamin programs should be avoided. A high-potency multi-vitamin provides needed support to a good diet. Other vitamins may be wasted because they are simply excreted from the body or cause harm. Some vitamins do not pass from the body and may be toxic if taken in larger quantities than a person's body requires.

DEVELOPING A PLAN FOR GOOD NUTRITION

Every educator should develop a plan for improving dietary habits. This does not mean that all bad habits or nutritional vices should be eliminated. Rather, the plan should focus on making one or two changes toward better nutrition. Once these changes have become routine, additional modifications may be made. This approach parallels advice given to dieters by nutritionists . . . it is better to lose weight slowly through calorie reduction than to lose it rapidly through fad diets. It is better to improve nutritional habits by modifying them slowly than to change all eating habits overnight.

Proper nutrition, combined with a program of regular exercise and stress control, can enable a person to live well into his or her nineties. One key to success is to make the plan to change eating habits a simple one. When a plan is too complex, the likelihood of sticking to it is slight. Simplicity will ensure greater success.

The following list provides some sample items for consideration in making a personal nutrition improvement plan. Common sense, consultation with a family physician, and books and literature will provide many other ideas.

1. When shopping, buy one or two fewer junk foods.
2. Eat a good breakfast at least 1 or 2 days each week (many nutritionists say that breakfast is the most important meal of the day and should be the largest).
3. Eat breakfast like a king, lunch like a prince, and supper like a pauper.
4. Stop eating 3 hours before going to bed, at least several days each week.
5. When going to a fast food restaurant for lunch, order a salad instead of the large hamburger. Order the small hamburger instead of the double burger, and the small french fries instead of the super size. Drink milk or juice instead of cola or coffee.

6. Drink decaffeinated coffee. Drink herb tea instead of coffee or regular tea at least 1 or 2 days a week.
7. Avoid shopping on an empty stomach.
8. Shop using a food list and stick to it. This prevents impulse buying. It saves money as well as calories.
9. Make one or two foods at home such as bread or salad dressing.
10. Use fried foods sparingly. Focus on baking and broiling as cooking methods.
11. Make vegetarian meals 1 or 2 days each week.
12. Reduce intake of red meats.
13. Keep a bowl of fresh vegetables prepared for snacking in the refrigerator in a clearly visible spot.
14. Avoid using the negative food items, such as sugar and salt, in cooking or keep them off the table whenever possible.
15. Keep a list of nutritional reminders attached to the front of the refrigerator.
16. Use whole wheat flour as often as possible in combination with white enriched flour.
17. Mix seltzer water with concentrated fruit juice to make a healthy soft drink instead of buying items packed with sugar and artificial ingredients.
18. Read food labels to buy items with the lowest amount of "danger" ingredients and additives.
19. Take a healthy lunch to school 1 or 2 days each week instead of buying a fast food or processed cafeteria meal.
20. Take healthy snacks and drinks to school to avoid using the candy, cake, and soft drink machines.

SUMMARY

The relationship between stress and nutrition is a concrete one. A person who is nutritionally deficient may succumb to illnesses and disorders that a person who follows proper dietary habits is able to avoid. When exposed to stress, the negative effects may be compounded for a person who is nutritionally weak.

A study by the Senate Select Committee on Nutrition and Human Needs identified that the average American's diet needs change. Recommended changes include greater consumption of fruits, vegetables, and whole grains; substituting lowfat dairy products for those with high fat content; reduction in consumption of saturated and animal fats; reduction in consumption of high cholesterol foods; and reduced consumption of foods with high sugar and salt content.

Nutritional habits affect people's actions. Students who eat poorly at lunch are often irritable, overactive, lethargic, or tense and nervous during afternoon classes. The classroom teacher deals with this situation every day.

The nutritional habits of many educators are poor. Teachers and administrators often follow a pattern of eating fast food and food fast. Educators also consume immoderate amounts of coffee, tea, cola, chocolate, and snack foods. Few educators practice what they preach as they inform students of the benefits of a well-balanced diet.

Maintaining a proper diet is neither too difficult nor expensive. It does not require a total change in eating patterns. It does require a commitment to self-improvement and to making a nutritional improvement plan.

One of the best steps to follow is eating a variety of foods. Foods should be eaten from each of the four food groups. Variety should be sought in fruits, vegetables, and grains.

Other guides to better nutrition include maintaining a healthy weight, avoiding too much fat and saturated fat, avoiding too much refined sugar, and avoiding too much salt and sodium. Before any steps are taken to reduce weight or alter eating habits, it is important to check with a physician. A physician can provide valuable assistance in identifying weaknesses and developing sound nutritional habits.

While much controversy surrounds the use of vitamins, data show that many people would benefit from taking a high-potency multivitamin every day. This provides nutrients that may be missed in a diet that does not include a variety of healthy foods. People should avoid self-prescribed vitamin therapy. Some vitamins are water soluble and are eliminated from the body in waste, but some are not eliminated and may be toxic if taken in the wrong amount.

Every educator should establish a personal nutrition improvement plan. The plan should be simple, focusing on only one or two changes. Once these are accomplished and the improvements become habit, additional changes may be pursued. A nutrition improvement plan will bring about positive change on a long-term basis. Such a plan requires commitment and initiative.

Diet alone can make a difference in how a person looks and feels. It also affects how a person responds to stress. When people feel good about themselves physically, other aspects of their life seem to fall into place. They are better able to cope with day-to-day stresses and strains. If they exercise regularly, in addition to maintaining a sound diet, the ability to control stress will be enhanced. The following chapter deals with physical development and exercise.

REFERENCES

Culligan, M., & Sedlacek, K. *How to kill stress before it kills you*. New York: Grosset & Dunlap, 1976.

McQuade, W., & Aikman, A. *Stress: What it is—What it can do to your health*. New York: E. P. Dutton, 1974.

Matteson & Ivancevich. *Managing job stress and health: The intelligent person's guide*. New York: The Free Press, 1982.

Shaffer, M. *Life after stress*. New York: Plenum Publishing Corp., 1982.

U.S. Department of Health, Education, and Welfare. *U.S. select committee report on nutrition and human needs*. Washington, DC: Department of Health, Education, and Welfare, 1977.

Winter, R. *Triumph over tension*. New York: Grosset & Dunlap, 1976.

Yates, J. E. *Managing stress*. New York: American Management Association, 1979.

Chapter 12

Exercise

As with nutrition, there is a direct link between stress and physical exercise. New theories and research abound. Health clubs have blossomed in almost every major city, county, and town in the nation.

Fitness is a major national concern. Businesses specializing in fitness products are growing rapidly. More people than ever before are making fitness programs a part of their daily routine. Despite this growth in fitness and the accompanying growth in standard of living, health problems continue to rise with many reaching epidemic proportions. For example, there has been little increase in the life expectancy of the American male in the past 20 years, while temporary and chronic illnesses and disabilities continue to grow in number. Over 28 million Americans have some degree of disability. In addition, the number of young people suffering from chronic conditions is increasing. Over 9 million children under the age of 15 have a chronic health problem. Business and industry lose billions of dollars annually to employees' health problems, causing a major financial and human drain to the economy.

James A. Lovell, astronaut and consultant to the President's Council on Physical Fitness and Sports, notes that while physicians are learning to cure more and more illnesses, 90% of the factors involving health care have little or nothing to do with members of the medical profession. Rather, individuals control their own health care. The primary threats to health and life in today's society are people's own sins of commission and omission. They smoke, eat too much, and exercise too little despite information provided by experts and researchers. Yet, the potential for improvement to overall health and well-being by modifying personal habits is unlimited (Katch, McArdle, & Boylan, 1979).

There is no better way to feel refreshed and positive, or experience personal achievement, than to participate in a vigorous physical workout. But, not everyone has the willpower or desire to jog 5 miles, play a set of tennis, swim 15 laps, or do a long series of stretching exercises upon awakening. Exercise is an individual undertaking. What is right and proper for one person may prove difficult and uncomfortable for another. For educators, for example, time constraints alone may interfere with implementing some of the exercise programs recommended by many leading authorities or best-selling books.

What a person does in the way of exercise is not as important as the effort made in doing something. The inactivity will prove far more harmful than the fact that the person is not doing the most up-to-date form of sit-ups or attending classes at the town's newest health club. A teacher, for example, will feel immediate gratification from taking a brief walk outdoors during a break between classes. The same teacher, if confined to a teacher's lounge to sip coffee and remain physically and mentally unproductive, will often feel fatigued or restless.

Activity is a biological necessity. Research has shown that unused muscles, brains, and other organs lose efficiency. To keep fit, educators must exercise their bodies as well as their minds. Inactivity deprives people of their need and ability to create and build, and this, in turn, causes tensions and insecurity that stem from aimlessness. Whether an educator considers activity to be work, relaxation, or play depends largely upon his or her attitude toward it. Selye (1974) suggests that people should get on friendly terms with their jobs, ideally finding "play professions" that are as pleasant, useful, and constructive as possible. Such jobs and professions allow for self-realization, and help to prevent irrational behavior, violent outbreaks, and escape to drugs and alcohol as sometimes occurs among people whose high motivation is frustrated. In seeking a worthwhile goal, educators should remember Selye's jingle: "Fight for your highest attainable aim, but never put up resistance in vain." In other words, it will never hurt to work hard for something an educator wants, but he or she must make sure that it is really what he or she wants and not merely a value or goal dictated by society, parents, teachers, or neighbors (Selye, 1974).

Developing and implementing a personal exercise program accomplishes several purposes. By emphasizing the *personal* nature of the effort, the opportunity for success is heightened. Even if the program is as simple as a brief daily walk, physical and emotional benefits may be realized. For the educator who recognizes that time and commitment allow only a few minutes a day for exercise, the rewards of a simple, daily walk could be as great as a long jog is to someone who has more time to devote to exercise. Conversely, a person with time constraints who attempts an exercise program that requires great lengths of time may find that the program creates more stress than it resolves. This is because the person has established an unattainable goal and has added to life's frustrations.

COMMITMENT TO A REGULAR PROGRAM

To gain full benefit from an exercise program, the program must be regular. This is the first commitment a person should make. Honesty in analyzing the available time, the nature of the exercise to be undertaken, and the benefits sought is a key to success.

Few educators get enough exercise. Daily activities often do not allow it or make it convenient. When this happens, it is necessary to establish a program of regular exercise despite the constraints of time. Quality of life and actual survival depend on it.

Most educators know that regular, virgorous exercise increases muscle strength and endurance. It also improves the functioning of the lungs, heart, and blood vessels, makes the joints more flexible, relieves tension, and helps lose and maintain weight. Medical research shows that people who are active have fewer heart attacks than those who are not. When active people do have heart attacks or become ill in other ways, they tend to recover more quickly (Stewart, 1979).

Many disorders are attributed to a lack of regular exercise. For example, more than half of all lower back pain has been linked to poor muscle tone in the back and lower abdomen. In many cases, lower back pain and related problems could be prevented or corrected through a program of regular exercise (Stewart, 1979).

There are many, many advantages to a regular exercise pattern. Again, this applies to those who exercise for only a few minutes each day, relying on simple activities such as walking or stretching, and to those who engage in more vigorous activity such as jogging, tennis, and swimming. Table 1 shows the advantages of a regular program of physical activity over a sedentary life-style.

The National Adult Physical Fitness Survey, conducted for the president's Council on Physical Fitness, revealed that 45% of all American adults do not

Table 1. Advantages of active vs. sedentary life-style

Area	Active	Sedentary
Weight	Low	High
Blood pressure	Low	High
Pulse rate	Low	High
Neuromuscular tension	Low	High
Muscular strength and flexibility	High	Low
Breathing capacity	High	Low
Adreno-cortical reserve	High	Low
Tiredness level	High	Low
Emotional stability	High	Low
Heart strength	High	Low
Aging	Late	Early

(Kraus, 1965).

exercise. Yet, those people who do not exercise quickly affirm their belief that they do get sufficient exercise. On the other hand, those people who do exercise regularly did not feel that they got all of the exercise they needed. Sixty-three percent of the nonexercisers said they got enough exercise during the course of a day, while only 53% of those who exercise regularly felt that they were as physically active as they should be. Of the 60 million Americans who do exercise regularly, nearly 45 million walk. This represents the largest segment of the exercising public. Compared to the walkers, 18 million exercisers ride bikes, 14 million swim, and 14 million do calisthenics (Opinion Research Corporation, 1972).

A regular program of physical exercise will help to reduce or eliminate fatigue. Inactivity over an extended period of time may lead to muscular atrophy. When this occurs, the body does not have enough physical strength to work or play efficiently. Regular exercise will increase the body's capability for performing normal, daily activities. Research also shows that a person who is physically fit uses less energy to perform routine movements than a person who is overweight or weak (Stewart, 1979).

Regular exercise will also strengthen a person's heart. Considering that heart attack is one of the greatest causes of premature death among human service workers (Greenberg & Valletutti, 1980), strengthening of the heart is one of the most important benefits to be derived from exercise. A study of 120,000 American railroad workers showed that the heart attack rate among office workers was approximately twice that of employees who worked in the yards where they were engaged in some regular physical activity.

Some research also shows that regular exercise can help develop resistance to degenerative disease and slow down the physical deterioration that comes with age. Not only can a regular exercise program possibly add years to a person's life, but it may also influence the quality of life. Proper exercise can make a person's later years more active and less burdened with illness and disorder (Stewart, 1979).

PHYSICAL EXAMINATION FIRST

Before beginning any exercise program, regardless of the nature of the exercise, a person should have a complete physical examination. Such an exam will explore the unknown factors that often cause difficulties once an exercise program is underway. The exam is important for all people, no matter how good or healthy they feel.

A physician will be able to detect illnesses in their early stage and prescribe proper treatment. If no illnesses are present, the physician can provide insight regarding the nature and extent of the exercise to be pursued. The examination will measure physical condition based on age, sex, weight, and health history. The doctor's information is invaluable in establishing an exercise program.

If needed, a physician will also prescribe nutritional changes. Beginning a diet to lose weight and initiating a strenuous exercise program at the same time may conflict and cause more harm than good. The dieting depletes the body of vital nutrients at a time when the exercise is causing increased demand for them. The result may range from feelings of weakness to serious disorders in the body's internal organs. A physician will provide advice on the best ways of balancing a proper program of weight loss with an effective exercise program.

The physician also needs to know what the person's exercise goals are. These should be provided in detail. Once the physician understands them, he or she can provide the proper advice. Too often, a person's exercise and weight control goals are not understood by the physician who then provides advice based simply on the person's current state of health and physical activity. When the physician's advice does not coincide with a person's specific goals, the advice is generally not taken. If both the physician and the individual have the same understanding of the purpose for exercise, full benefit will be derived from the examination and advice.

SPECIFIC ASPECTS OF FITNESS

Physical fitness is much more than a healthy-looking physique. In fact, many people with trim, muscular bodies are unhealthy. Their body type gives them a lean appearance, but they may lack strength, agility, endurance, and other aspects of good health and fitness.

Physical fitness has been defined in many ways. Generally, it is a state of well-being that permits a person to enjoy life to the fullest. It has also been defined as the general capacity to adapt and respond favorably to physical effort (Federal Bureau of Investigation, 1972). Fitness has also been described as the ability to perform certain actions, including running, jumping, dodging, falling, climbing, swimming, riding, lifting and carrying heavy loads, and enduring long hours of continuous work. The six aspects of motor fitness are balance, flexibility, agility, strength, power, and endurance. A good exercise program will focus on all six aspects of motor fitness. A brief description of each aspect follows.

Balance

Good balance is important because it enables a person to use full physical potential. It is the result of neuromuscular control, which occurs when muscles and nerves work together in the performance of certain movements and skills. People with poor balance are often accident prone because of poor body control. Balance can be improved through a variety of exercises.

Flexibility

Flexibility is related to the ability to move the many joints in the human body. Flexible joints provide a wide range of movement while stiff ones result in restriction. In many cases, loss of flexibility is one of the first signs of physical deterioration.

Agility

Agility involves the ability to react quickly with controlled body movements. It enables a person to cope with a situation quickly with a minimum of injury. Agility is essential to such activities as tennis, climbing ladders, dodging obstacles, etc.

Strength

Strength is simply a person's ability to exert force. It is essential to daily functioning. Strength in arms and hands is vital for lifting objects. Strength in legs and feet is needed for walking and standing. Strength in the trunk and back is needed for routine lifting. A lack of strength inhibits the performance of many daily tasks.

Power

Power is the explosive force that enables the body to move suddenly or propel an object. Power is required to run sprints or throw a heavy object.

Endurance

Endurance is the capacity for continued exertion over a prolonged period of time. It involves the rapid supply of oxygen to working muscles and is necessary for such tasks as running, swimming, walking long distances quickly, and bicycling. Endurance is regarded as the prime factor in determining fitness and is given more emphasis than balance, flexibility, agility, strength, and power.

Boyer and Kasch (1968) have identified two components of physical fitness: cardiovascular fitness and musculoskeletal fitness. Cardiovascular fitness involves effective functioning of the heart and blood vessels, while musculoskeletal fitness pertains to effective functioning of the muscles, joints, and bone structure including such body mechanics as posture, balance, flexibility, alignment, movement, and the release of musculoskeletal tensions.

FITNESS AND EDUCATORS

Many educators exert a great deal of physical energy during the course of the average workday. The elementary school teacher who is on his or her feet all day and the college professor running from one building to another both expend significant energy. But, their efforts work only a small group of muscles and there is little or no pattern to their "exercise."

While most educators work a few muscle groups extensively, their overall physical activity is only slight to moderate. For some, the work environment is sedentary. The job requires only moderate movement and there is very little activity requiring use of various muscle groups.

When educators leave their school for the day, most go home and collapse into an easy chair or immediately begin their personal chores. Then, they focus on preparing lessons, grading papers, or preparing reports for the next day. The percentage of educators who engage in vigorous exercise on a daily basis is small.

In interviews with elementary and high school teachers and school board administrators, the two primary excuses for their failure to exercise were lack of time and fatigue. The excuse of no time is valid when thinking of an exercise program that requires a commitment of an hour or two every day. But many opportunities exist to exercise in such a way as to require only minutes each day. Again, each individual must judge his or her own limitations and commitment to exercise and should approach the amount of time available realistically. If 15 minutes is available, the program should be developed with this in mind.

On the surface, fatigue, the second excuse, seems a valid one. After a long day teaching in the classroom or dealing with personnel matters, an educator may feel so mentally exhausted that drawing on the body's energy reserve to exercise seems impossible. Yet, exercise is a proven means for combating fatigue and its effects.

Fatigue is the result of an accumulation of metabolic waste products in overworked cells. It results in lower efficiency, irritability, emotional stress, and feelings of tiredness. When mental and physical fatigue are caused by overwork or complex work, rest is needed to allow the body to rid itself of the accumulated wastes. But, fatigue is not always caused by overwork. More often, it is caused by lack of activity and diversion. Rather than overactivity, it is underactivity, and its accompanying sluggish circulation and lack of glandular stimulation that causes the fatigue (Vitale, 1973).

BASIC PRINCIPLES FOR A CONDITIONING PROGRAM

Regardless of the type of exercises chosen, several basic principles should be followed to ensure that a self-conditioning program will work.

Create a Total Fitness Program

There is no single exercise or activity that develops all muscle groups and ensures total fitness. A person should select a program of exercise that is both comfortable and designed to develop all parts of the body. Special emphasis should be placed on developing those parts of the body that are particularly weak or deficient. A program limited to jogging will improve cardiovascular fitness but will do little for arms, shoulders, and the trunk area. Weight lifting will work the upper body but will do little for cardiovascular endurance. Any exercise or fitness program should include exercises that focus on cardiovascular endurance, muscular strength and endurance, and flexibility.

Cardiovascular Endurance Cardiovascular endurance involves the heart's ability to perform at a higher level than usual, for a prolonged period of time and with efficiency. It also involves a rapid recovery upon cessation of the activity. Exercises for this include running, jogging, swimming, cycling, and others requiring rapid oxygen flow and heavy breathing.

Muscular Strength and Endurance Muscular endurance is the ability of muscles to either maintain maximum contraction or to contract repetitively for a relatively long period of time. Strength is the ability of muscles to contract and overcome resistance. Exercises in this area include weight lifting, push-ups, pull-ups, sit-ups, isometrics, and working with heavy objects such as medicine balls.

Flexibility Flexibility involves the range of motion of the joints. It can be improved through exercises that incorporate stretching, bending, and twisting movements.

Warm Up First . . . Then Cool Down

To ensure success, a good teacher prepares himself or herself before beginning a lesson. Similarly, an educator should prepare before exercising. The purpose of a warm-up is to protect against injuries and a sudden development of oxygen deficiency. Warming up involves performing gradual, light, rhythmic exercises before more strenuous activity is begun. Walking, bending, stretching, and running in place are sound warm-up exercises. Once vigorous exercise has been completed, the same amount of time allotted to the warm-up should be spent cooling down, again relying on less strenuous activities such as walking or stretching. The cool-down allows muscles to relax and blood to return to internal organs. It also allows respiration to return to normal. In any exercise program, there should be a gradual acceleration of activity, a peak output, then a gradual deceleration.

Determine Tolerance and Progression Levels

For exercise to be effective, it must be the right type and the right amount. A person should determine his or her own tolerance level, i.e., the level at which the body responds favorably to exercise. An exercise program that is too easy or puts too much strain on the body will be of little value. It is equally important to determine how progress will be made. Maximum fitness cannot be attained overnight. Some strain and soreness is normal in the beginning, but, when this reaches the point of causing a person to lose sleep, feel ill, or experience sore muscles for many days, the exercise has been overdone. As fitness improves, exercise can be made more strenuous. In time, the body will adapt beautifully to the demands made on it.

Work All Parts of the Body

Even if the objective is to concentrate on a specific weakness such as a wide mid-section, it is important to work all muscle groups and all parts of the body. Every exercise session, regardless of duration, should focus on the upper and lower body and should include cardiovascular endurance, muscular strength, and flexibility exercises.

Practice Deep Breathing

Deep breathing aids circulation and helps to prevent fatigue. Deep breathing should be practiced during warm-ups, peak exercise, and cool-downs. Holding the breath during exercise should be avoided.

Recuperate

In addition to doing light exercises at the end of a session, it is important to recuperate. This involves continuous movement of some sort, such as walking, until the rate of perspiration is reduced. Once this occurs, a person can take a shower, sit, or relax. Going from strenuous exercise to a shower without allowing time for relaxation and recuperation should be avoided (Federal Bureau of Investigation, 1972).

EXERCISES

Most libraries have a bountiful supply of books that provide guidelines on specific exercises. Anyone interested in starting a regular exercise program should review some of these texts to learn about the large variety of activities available. It is important, if the exercise program is to be successful, that the activities suit the individual's needs.

There are different categories of exercises, providing choices on how to warm up, improve endurance, build strength, increase flexibility, and achieve relaxation. To show the variety of exercises available, some of the choices are listed below.

1. *Warm-up exercises*
   a) Leg bends
   b) Arm, leg, and body stretches
   c) Leg raises
   d) Head and neck rotations
   e) Side twists and bends
   f) Walking
2. *Endurance exercises*
   a) Walking
   b) Jogging
   c) Swimming
   d) Bicycling
   e) Dancing
   f) Skipping rope

     g) Doing jumping jacks
3. *Strength exercises*
     a) Weight lifting
     b) Knee bends
     c) Push-ups
     d) Side leg raises
4. *Flexibility exercises*
     a) Toe touching
     b) Body stretching
     c) Single leg raises
     d) Calf and achilles tendon stretches
     e) Side bends
     f) Head rotations
     (Halper & Neiger, 1980)

Aerobic Exercise

There are many programs that offer enjoyable ways to participate in aerobic exercise with other people. Jazzercize and Aerobicize courses are offered by many colleges, YMCAs, YWCAs, recreation and parks departments, and private companies. They offer the opportunity to get together with neighbors, friends, and new acquaintances, all of whom are seeking to improve their health and well-being.

One of the benefits of these programs, in addition to the participation of a group of people, is the relaxed, enjoyable approach offered by instructors. They tend to make the programs fun, supported by comfortably paced music. Many people prefer these programs to the more tedious or competitive aerobic exercises of running, racketball, biking, etc.

TIPS FOR EXERCISING MORE EFFECTIVELY

Halper and Neiger (1980), in their research on exercise and fitness, developed a list of helpful tips for people planning an exercise program. People should choose those items from the list that best suit their own needs.

1. Exercise with neighbors, friends, a spouse, or children. The family dog may also serve as a companion on a walk or jog.
2. Change exercise routines to provide variety.
3. Light competition may be an incentive to some people.
4. Exercise to music.
5. For people who have trouble sleeping, exercise before going to bed.
6. Establish a reward system, allowing a prize of some sort for successful accomplishment. This aids in breaking up the boredom of exercise.

7. Maintain records on the exercise program and keep track of accomplishments.
8. Be positive. A day missed is not reason for calamity.
9. If one exercise routine does not work, others should be explored and tried.
10. Gym equipment is unnecessary. Exercise does not have to be expensive.
11. The exercise program should be simple. Complexity may lead to discouragement with the routine.
12. The exercise routine should be regular, a part of every day's activities.
13. Progression should be gradual for full benefits to be realized.
14. Breaks in the routine should be taken whenever desired. This aids in reducing harmful body strain.
15. Goals should be established and ranked in order of their importance. This will help a person stay on track in his or her program.
16. Age is not a barrier to exercise.
17. A person should learn to recognize the difference between moderation and strain.
18. The exercise program should be organized so that it fits comfortably into the daily schedule.
19. A 10-minute cool down period should follow any good exercise program.
20. Exercise in hot, humid weather should be avoided. It can cause dehydration and a dangerous elevation in body temperature.
21. Exercising should not occur for at least one hour after a meal.
22. The ability to perform exercise can vary from day to day. This should be recognized and more frequent breaks should be taken on those days when exercise requires greater strain.
23. Alcohol and exercise do not mix and this combination should be avoided. Alcohol dilates body vessels, diverting blood from the muscles where the oxygen is needed most.
24. Smoking elevates heart rate, lowers the capacity of the blood to carry oxygen, reduces breathing efficiency, and reduces flow of blood to the muscles and heart.
25. It is important to be as fit as possible for a person's age. It is not important for all people to be as fit as a 20-year-old athlete (Halper & Neiger, 1980).

Other helpful tips to make exercising more effective, efficient, and enjoyable can be obtained through reading, from physicians, friends, family members, and exercise instructors. Any source available should be tapped to establish the best possible personal exercise program.

WALKING

There are many exercises that aid in alleviating the harmful effects of stress. The simple process of walking deserves specific mention. It offers many benefits with minimal risk or preparation.

Walking is being recognized by more and more physicians as an effective exercise. In hospitals, many physicians now attempt to have their patients walk as soon as possible after surgery. By doing so, deaths from embolism, which is a sudden blockage of the blood vessels, have been reduced significantly (Johnson, 1980).

Walking is particularly beneficial for people who are overweight, out of shape, or inactive. Walking regularly and purposefully over a period of time trims the body and strengthens and tones the muscles. It provides a sound way to prepare for more vigorous exercise and serves as an excellent supplement to other exercises. In addition, walking does not cause the pounding and shock to the body common in such exercises as jogging or running. Yet, many of its benefits are the same. Walking can improve cardiovascular and respiratory functions, increase energy levels, and reduce fat in the body.

Walking as an exercise is different from taking a casual stroll around the neighborhood, although any walk is better than no walk at all. For full benefits to be realized, walking should be regular and vigorous. Halper and Neiger (1980) offer a simple program for starting a walking routine:

Phase I—Walk at an easy pace for 5 minutes.
Phase II—Walk at a brisk pace that is not too tiring for 10 minutes. (If breathlessness occurs, the pace should be slowed.)
Phase III—Walk at an easy pace for 5 minutes.

This program should be followed for one week, walking every day if possible. During the second week, the brisk walk should be increased to 15 minutes. During the third week, the brisk walk should be increased to 20 minutes. The first and last 5 minutes of relaxed walking should always serve as the warm-up and cool-down period. After the third week, one of the following alternatives may be considered: a) the distance walked should be increased during each session, b) a vigorous 20-minute walk should be done twice each day, c) other exercises should be added to the program, or d) the pace of the third week should be maintained for a while.

There are some general tips on walking that may prove helpful to anyone considering a program.

—Comfortable, well-supported, low-heeled shoes should be worn, along with absorbent socks.
—The walk should be as long and far as time will allow without feeling discomfort.
—A brisk pace should be maintained for 20 minutes. (Walking one mile in 20 minutes will burn 100 calories.)
—Sustained activity is important, regardless of the initial pace. It is important to walk at least three times during the first week, and more if possible.
—Walking with someone else may make the time pass quickly and add another

dimension to the program. Even with another person, though, the vigorous pace should be maintained.

—If the walk is on hilly terrain, warm-up and cool-down should occur on as level an area as possible.

Walking and Educators

Walking is an excellent exercise for educators. It can be accomplished before, after, or during the school day. A walk around the school grounds during a break (away from areas where students and others are congregating) is an excellent refresher. A long walk during lunch improves physical well-being, mental attitude, and emotional feelings. A walk immediately after work helps to separate the school day from home and family life.

Walking provides exposure to the simple pleasures of life, particularly during certain seasons of the year. The simple beauties of nature help to balance the complexities of the classroom or educational administration. A brief, vigorous walk also helps to suppress appetite. (A 3- or 4-minute walk before a meal may be more beneficial as an appetite suppressant than the most expensive diet pills.)

A walk at the end of the workday with a friend or spouse provides an excellent time to discuss the stresses and strains of the workday. It creates an environment for positive information sharing. During a walk, both the speaker and the listener communicate more effectively than they would in a more complex, stressful setting. There are few interruptions or other people to interfere during a walk.

RESULTS OF EXERCISING

Some of the advantages of an exercise program were previously cited. There are many others. An educator who engages in a regular exercise program will recognize and feel immediate results. Some soreness will occur as unused muscles and tendons are stretched and pulled, lungs work harder, and the heart beats faster. But, a sense of genuine accomplishment will be realized right away. In addition, mental and emotional strain and tension seem to disappear almost immediately upon engaging in an aerobic exercise activity. Generally, a regular exercise program that follows the basic principles set forth in this chapter will enable a person to prevent stress-related disease and cope more effectively with the stresses and strains of daily life. Some of the physiological and subjective benefits that may be realized include:

1. Decreased heart (pulse) rate (based on participation in vigorous exercise done over a period of several months or more)
2. Reduced blood pressure (also based on prolonged and vigorous exercise)
3. Increased oxygen intake and improved breathing efficiency

4. Decreased serum cholesterol
5. More effective utilization of carbohydrates
6. Less adrenaline and noradrenaline released by the body in response to psychological stress
7. Lower likelihood of clot formation in blood vessels
8. Increased flexibility of blood vessels, decreasing the tendency toward atherosclerotic patches
9. Possible increased diameter of existing coronary arteries
10. Improved muscular strength
11. Increased muscle tone and flexibility
12. Improved stamina and physical endurance
13. Increased nutrient exchange at the tissue level
14. Improved digestion
15. Better overall appearance as a result of weight gain, loss, or distribution
16. Decreased appetite, assisting in loss of excess weight
17. Improved complexion (usually the result of improved circulation)
18. Better posture
19. Improved general attitude and frame of mind
20. Increased feelings of tranquility and improved relaxation
21. Subsequent muscle relaxation
22. Improved thinking
23. Delays in the aging process
24. Prevention of minor backaches
25. Improved self-esteem and self-image (Morse & Furst, 1979)

RECOMMENDATION

Whether in an urban elementary school or a major university, an exercise group can be started. Each day, a group of teachers and administrators can get together during their lunch period to walk. If time and facilities allow, they may meet in the gymnasium to participate in some aerobics or calisthenics. They may decide to meet before or after work to participate in a program.

In schools where such groups have been formed, success has been high. Exercise groups provide incentive. They also provide a chance for teachers and administrators to meet casually and get to know one another in a nonbusiness type of setting. In addition, physical education instructors have served as guides to such groups, offering expertise that might not otherwise be available.

The following chapters offer additional ways to reduce and manage stress as it relates to the field of education. The techniques should be used in conjunction with, and not in place of, a regular exercise program. This approach will provide a well-rounded means for coping with and preventing the harmful effects of stress and will greatly improve the chances for success.

SUMMARY

The impact of regular exercise on reducing and coping more effectively with the stresses and strains of daily life is dramatic. Exercise maintains fitness and efficiency. It prevents many of the illnesses and diseases often associated with stress, tension, and anxiety.

It is important for an educator to set aside some time for activities related to exercise and physical well-being. The process of doing something on a regular basis is as important as the nature of the exercise chosen. An exercise program should be personal; that is, it should be pleasing and manageable to the individual educator. A program deemed effective by one person may be very uncomfortable to another.

Commitment to a *regular* exercise program is essential. An occasional participation in a physical activity on a weekend is insufficient. Such activity may prove harmful. A regular program, however, will improve the functioning of the lungs, heart, blood vessels, joints, and more. Medical data show that people who engage in regular exercise programs have fewer heart attacks, less back pain, and fewer problems with maintaining ideal weight. Regular exercise also helps to reduce fatigue and improves a person's capability to perform daily routines.

Any exercise program should begin with a physical examination or, at least, a consultation with a physician. The goals of the program should be discussed. The physician may offer tips on exercise programs, warnings on those to avoid, and guidelines for dietary changes to accompany the program.

A good exercise program will focus on six aspects of motor fitness: balance, flexibility, agility, strength, power, and endurance. Each of these areas is important to overall well-being. A well-rounded exercise program will include activities from each of these areas.

Because of their workday and the demands made upon them, many educators do not exercise. In general, 40% of the public does not exercise. Fatigue is one of the major reasons given by teachers and school administrators for not exercising. Yet, regular exercise helps to overcome fatigue. The lack of time available to educators for participation in an exercise program can also be overcome with little difficulty.

The basic principles for any regular exercise program include:

1. Creating a total fitness program, with attention to cardiovascular fitness, muscular strength and endurance, and flexibility
2. Warming up before participating in vigorous exercise and cooling down once the program is completed.
3. Determining personal tolerance and progression levels (a program that is effective for one person may be uncomfortable and ineffective for another)
4. Working all parts of the body

5. Practicing deep breathing before, during, and after the exercise (this is also helpful as a relaxation technique at any time)
6. Recuperating once the exercise program is complete

There are many benefits to a regular exercise program. A person's overall physical well-being is improved. In addition, regular exercise improves mental and emotional well-being.

There are many exercises from which an educator may implement a personal fitness program. Tips for making the program successful range from having clearly established goals to creating a reward system (the same type of positive reinforcement educators use with their students). Of the many exercises available, walking is one that requires a minimum of skill and preparation while providing substantial benefit. Walking requires regular, vigorous activity. It can be accomplished during the school day, during breaks and during lunch periods, or in the evening with a friend or spouse. It improves physical health and offers an opportunity for mental and emotional conditioning as well.

Because of the stresses and strains associated with the field of education, participation in a regular exercise program is important to all teachers and administrators. It provides benefits not realized in any other stress-management techniques. It helps people look and feel better, regardless of their current state. There is no substitute for a regular exercise program in the battle against the negative effects of stress.

REFERENCES

Boyer, J., & Kasch, F. *Adult fitness—Principles and practices.* Greeley, CO: All American Productions and Publications, 1968.

Federal Bureau of Investigation. *Physical fitness for L.E. officers.* Washington, DC: United States Department of Justice, 1972.

Greenberg, S. F., & Valletutti, P. J. *Stress and the helping professions.* Baltimore: Paul H. Brookes Publishing Co., 1980.

Halper, M. S., & Neiger, I. *Physical fitness.* New York: Holt, Rinehart & Winston, 1980.

Johnson, H. J. *Creative walking for physical fitness.* New York: Grosset & Dunlap, 1980.

Katch, F., McArdle, W., & Boylan, B. *Getting in shape.* Boston: Houghton Mifflin Co., 1979.

Kraus, H. *Backache, stress and tension: Cause, prevention and treatment.* New York: Simon and Schuster, 1965.

Morse, D. R., & Furst, M. L. *Stress for success.* New York: VanNostrand Reinhold Co., 1979.

Opinion Research Corporation. *Adult Physical Fitness Survey* (For the President's Council on Physical Fitness). Princeton, NJ, 1972.

Selye, H. *Stress without distress.* Philadelphia: J. B. Lippincott, 1974.

Stewart, P. *U.S. fitness book.* New York: Simon and Schuster, 1979.

Vitale, F. *Individualized fitness programs.* Englewood Cliffs, NJ: Prentice-Hall, 1973.

Chapter 13

Relaxation

Many people are unable to relax. They are tense and tired, feel edgy at home and work, lose their temper often, and generally feel stressed. Busy people of high intelligence and those who are very sensitive are most susceptible to this pattern of behavior. These people are also susceptible to physical harm because of their inability to relax. Common physical ailments include chest pains, stomach pains, ulcers, asthma, and skin disorders.

Dale Carnegie, author of *How to Stop Worrying and Start Living* (1974), states that relaxation is the answer to nervous fatigue. Educators should learn to relax while doing their work. For most, this requires that they reverse the habits of a lifetime. But it is worth the effort since it may lead to a more enjoyable life! Tension is a habit. Relaxing is a habit. Bad habits can be broken. Good habits can be formed (Carnegie, 1974).

RELAXATION AND NERVES

When educators experience stress, their nervous system "overworks." Their pulse, respiration rate, and blood pressure generally climb. A cycle begins in which they feel pressure, and the sense of pressure causes them to become frustrated. This, in turn, creates additional stress. Unless stopped, the cycle continues and stress mounts to the point of becoming disruptive.

In relaxation, the nervous system takes charge and depresses the harmful effects of stress. Respiration and blood pressure are reduced. Following relaxation, the individual returns to a state and sense of equilibrium (Sehnert, 1981). Medical researchers have identified relaxation as a primary means for coping with high blood pressure and its consequences.

CHOOSING RELAXATION TECHNIQUES

The development of good relaxation habits should not be taken for granted. The physical, mental, and emotional rewards for relaxing make it one of the best investments in health and stress reduction that a person can pursue. The feelings most people have after a period of relaxation are generally favorable. Attitude and mental awareness improve. Coping with stress seems easier. Interaction with others, whether at home or in the school, is positive.

How an educator relaxes is personal, as unique to the individual as hobbies and style of dress. Some people get pleasure from sitting in an easy chair and listening to soft music on the stereo. For others, sitting for long periods listening to soft music is stressful. Some enjoy meditating for relaxation, while others prefer taking a walk.

Time is a factor in relaxing. Some educators claim that they do not have time to relax. While some time is required, a great deal of relaxation can be realized in a very short period. The following list represents some of the relaxation techniques available to educators. Most can be accomplished in a brief period of time, while others require considerable time. Some techniques can be accomplished in less time than it takes for a quick coffee break. A brief summary of each technique listed below is provided in the remainder of this chapter.

1. Meditation
2. Biofeedback
3. Self-hypnosis
4. Massage
5. Warm bath and pampering
6. Physical exercise
7. Time alone
8. Music
9. Hobbies
10. Short vacations
11. Time with friends

Meditation

Meditation is simply a mental escape from daily routine. It is a relaxation technique in which an educator reduces blood pressure and the need for oxygen through a calm, restful thought process. Meditation is becoming widely accepted in the United States as a means for relaxing and reducing stress. Transcendental meditation (TM) is one of the more popular meditation techniques. Once mastered, meditation provides relaxation in a short amount of time. The person practicing meditation seeks a calm, quiet environment. For an educator, a quiet corner of a faculty lounge or an empty classroom would suffice. At home, an easy chair, bed, or soft carpet in a quiet room is excellent.

Dr. Herbert Benson, author of *The Relaxation Response,* offers the following guidelines for practicing the technique of meditation. The teacher or administrator practicing meditation as a stress-reduction technique sits in a comfortable position. Eyes remain closed and breathing becomes deep, slow, and steady.

External thoughts are pushed aside and the mind is cleared of work and home related matters. This can be accomplished by repeating a special word or phrase (known as a *mantra*) over and over to direct the mind away from the normal, often stressful mental process (Benson, 1975).

Meditation should (initially) last for about 20 minutes. After mastering the technique, the same benefits can be realized in a shorter period of time. Some people practice meditation twice daily, usually once in the morning and once in the evening. In the beginning, two times a day is recommended.

There are many benefits to meditation. Studies at Harvard University and the University of California show that a person's need for oxygen and rate of metabolism are reduced during meditation. Studies also indicate that, during meditation, the person's brain patterns are at rest. It provides a feeling of comfort and relaxation, often helping a person to become refreshed.

People who practice meditation say that it improves memory and learning. It aids in maintaining emotional stability, although this has not been supported scientifically. There is sufficient evidence available to support meditation as a way to achieve emotional and physiological benefits (Winter, 1976).

Research shows that during meditation the average person's metabolic rate is generally reduced to a level below that of the deepest sleep. Oxygen consumption decreases to 20% below that for a night's sleep. Cardiac output falls to 25% below that experienced during normal waking hours, while it decreases only 20% during sleep. All of this leads to the conclusion that meditation provides a level of relaxation and rejuvenation that exceeds normal sleep. It is a heightened state of restfulness, yet the mind remains alert (Anderson, 1978).

Anderson (1978) and Benson (1975) recommend the following basic techniques for meditating. An educator should:

1. Find a quiet place where there will be no disturbances and where a relaxed position can be obtained without falling asleep. This position may be sitting on the floor with legs crossed or sitting in a firm chair, holding the spine erect, with feet flat on the ground.
2. Consciously relax the neck, back, shoulders, and abdomen as much as possible at the outset. Breathing gently in and out will help. Saying the same word, such as "relax" or "let go," repeatedly will also be helpful.
3. Continue the process, consciously relaxing the muscles and the entire body, then the emotion, and then the mind.
4. Direct thoughts to a theme. This may begin with a simple phrase such as "I seek peaceful relationships," or may be stimulated by imagining a beautiful or tranquil place.
5. Continue this process. If the mind strays away from the theme, turn thoughts back to it. Continue directing thoughts toward the theme.
6. Relax for whatever amount of time is available.

For some, meditation can take place in 10 to 20 minutes. Initially, people may have to spend more time on it until the process becomes comfortable. In any case, the person derives from the process feelings of physical, mental, and emotional refreshment.

Biofeedback

Stress tends to raise blood pressure and heart rate and increase muscular tension. It may cause sweating and feelings of extreme heat or chills. Biofeedback (from the words *biological feedback*) involves controlling these and other bodily functions through the thought process. The mind controls the body as thoughts cause blood pressure level to drop, body temperature to change, and muscles to relax. The technique relies on equipment that measures such things as heart rate, blood pressure, brain waves, and skin temperature. Many physicians, psychiatrists, and psychologists now rely heavily on biofeedback machines to aid their patients and clients. Some maintain large-scale biofeedback laboratories.

Like meditation and other relaxation techniques, biofeedback requires practice (Culligan & Sedlacek, 1976). The equipment is attached to the individual to measure specific muscle groups, temperature through the fingers, etc. It is simple and painless. The person then practices relaxation techniques and receives immediate feedback. As the state of relaxation increases, the teacher or administrator sees his or her blood pressure decrease. This serves as a teaching technique for helping to learn the process that best addresses a particular bodily function. It also provides immediate positive reinforcement to the learner.

In a short while, an educator can proceed without the equipment. She or he knows how to reduce high blood pressure or muscular tension. At various intervals, the educator may return to the equipment to evaluate progress and sharpen the relaxation skills.

Biofeedback equipment is expensive. Most people rely on their physician, employee assistance program, or counseling service to provide biofeedback instruction. Such professional assistance should be sought because of the complexity of the equipment.

Self-Hypnosis

Dr. Herbert Spiegel, of Columbia University, one of the world's leading authorities on scientific uses of hypnosis, states that a close parallel exists between meditation, biofeedback, self-hypnosis, and other techniques that require an attentive, narrowed concentration to ease or erase external distractions as a means for relaxation (McQuade & Aikman, 1974). He champions the use of hypnosis as a technique for reducing stress and addressing the problems that underlie it.

Woolfolk and Richardson (1978) define hypnosis as the altered state of consciousness that results from focusing attention on a set of suggestions and allowing oneself to be receptive to those suggestions, thereby allowing free reign to one's powers of imagination.

Use of self-hypnosis is a simple technique that can be easily mastered, again with practice. There are several techniques for inducing self-hypnosis. An educator interested in the subject should research some of the texts available on the topic or contact a local counseling service. The following is a summary of one self-hypnosis technique.

One of the most common methods for inducing self-hypnosis is termed *eye fixation*. This technique requires an individual to:

1. Select a spot with minimum distraction, although silence and lack of human traffic are not essential to hypnosis.
2. Sit in a comfortable position, much the same as for meditation.
3. Stare at a stationary object.
4. While concentrating on the object, "silently tell yourself that your eyelids are getting heavier and heavier and that pretty soon they will close and you will feel very relaxed, yet fully aware" (Yates, 1979).
5. Repeat this suggestion every minute or so until relaxation begins.
6. During the process, breathe slowly and deeply, holding the breath every now and then and exhaling very slowly.
7. During the breathing, repeat a special word such as "relax" or "peace" or "joy."

Once relaxation is obtained, a person can give himself or herself some simple suggestions, known as autosuggestion. Yates (1979) gives six guidelines for autosuggestion:

1. The more often a suggestion is repeated, the more effective it will be.
2. Suggestions should always be stated in positive terms.
3. Progress should be anticipated in small stages. Rapid, sudden changes rarely occur in hypnosis. Suggestions should, therefore, be simple.
4. The power of positive thinking is important. People should realize that physical, mental, and emotional improvement can be obtained through self-hypnosis and that chances for success are good.
5. Autosuggestions should be stated in statements rather than commands. "I choose to . . ." should be used instead of "I must. . . ." People resist taking orders from anyone, including themselves.
6. During self-hypnosis, a person should visualize himself or herself as relaxed. Creating a picture image is helpful. This imagery aids in ensuring success of the self-hypnosis process.

There is no risk of harm in self-hypnosis. Despite the image given to hypnosis by theatrical and stage performers, it is a safe process. The educator who tries it will neither sleep nor lose control. The process can be ended at any time, simply by opening the eyes and stating, "I want to end this process." It has been shown to be an effective, quick, and simple relaxation technique as well as a means for self-improvement (Greenberg & Valletutti, 1980). Self-hypnosis, like other meditation techniques, is well suited to a classroom or office environment. It can be used quickly and effectively to achieve heightened relaxation, even during times of stress and strain. A clinical psychologist stated that he is able to achieve the equivalent of a 2-hour nap in about 15 minutes using self-hypnosis.

Massage

One of the best, and most frequently overlooked, ways to relax is a good massage. Manipulating tense, tight muscles relaxes them and therefore relaxes the individual (Winter, 1976). Massage is soothing, calming, and enjoyable. It can be provided by a professional masseur or masseuse at a health club, or by a friend or relative.

A number of good books available at book stores and local libraries provide instruction on massage. There are several books on the benefits of massage for children as well as for adults. If no one is available to give a massage, a person can manipulate his or her muscles into a relaxed state. From toes to forehead, a person can knead the various muscle groups causing the tension in them to be reduced or eliminated.

Warm Bath and Pampering

For many years, medical science has known about the benefits of hydrotherapy. Patients have been relaxed by resting in warm water. Historically, the benefits of a warm bath were espoused by the ancient Romans (Winter, 1976). Yet, many people ignore this relaxation technique.

The amount of time it takes to rest in a warm tub of water is worthwhile because of the many benefits. Yet, most educators will rush through a shower in order to save a few minutes. A soak in a warm bath, particularly one to which bath salts or scented lotions have been added, is a proven relaxation technique. Many physicians prescribe warm baths to patients who suffer from stiff necks and backaches.

One technique involves running the bath water to body temperature, as close to 98.6° as possible. A regular thermometer can be used as a guide. Time in the tub should last for 10 to 30 minutes. Then, the person should towel himself or herself dry and immediately rest in bed for another 10–30 mintues. The result is a heightened state of relaxation for an investment of only 20 minutes to 1 hour.

Time Alone

The benefit of time alone every day can not be underemphasized as a relaxation technique. This is particularly important for those educators who have large families or many commitments outside of their school activities.

There are teachers who wake up in the morning and assist family members in getting their day started. They then face a classroom of students, and interact with parents, administrators, and support personnel. Upon arriving home, the tasks of the household may seem insurmountable. There may be a spouse and children who need and deserve attention, as well as chores to be performed. Then, there may be lessons to grade, reports to review, and parents or students to call. Unless a commitment is made to taking time for self, time alone is not possible.

Time alone can be spent reading or just sitting quietly. It may be spent talking to a friend or participating in any of the relaxation techniques mentioned in this chapter. It may last for 15 minutes or 2 hours, whatever is desired, and can be gained without creating too much additional stress. Whatever the length and regardless of how the time is spent, it should occur at least once each day. It is the person's special time to reflect, think, rest, cry, laugh, or do whatever is personally needed at the time.

Music

"Music hath charms. . . ." is the beginning of an old saying that many people know but few follow. Tastes in music are as individual as tastes in food, clothes, cars, and homes. Most people find joy and relaxation in listening to their favorite music on the stereo or radio. Whether it's country, classical, popular, or easy listening, music tends to have a calming effect on its fans. When taking time alone, a person can listen to music. When taking a brief break in the faculty lounge, a teacher can listen to a radio. While sitting and grading papers in the evining, music can be playing in the background.

The benefits of music should not be overlooked. But, certain precautions should be taken. Loud noise can create stress so it is important to keep the background music at a low volume. Some rock and "new wave" music has been found to have a stressful effect on people. It should be avoided as a stress reducer. When there is conversation, particularly with a group of people, background music can be an annoyance and may create unnecessary stress. In general, though, music in the proper atmosphere offers an enjoyable way to relax and reduce the stresses and strains of the day.

Hobbies

Most educators have hobbies. Even those who do not have typical hobbies have interests toward which they would like to devote more time. Hobbies offer a pleasant way to reduce stress. Most hobbies have reinforcers built into them. When a piece of antique furniture is refinished or an engine is rebuilt or the last piece is placed on a homemade dress, the rewards go beyond those realized during the process. The teacher or administrator who sews may find great relaxation in the time spent at the sewing machine or in doing the handwork. At the end of the process is a new suit or coat to be enjoyed.

Many educators who had hobbies as children and teenagers abandoned them for the demands of adulthood and their profession. They often wish they had the time to return to their stamp collecting or model trains or family geneology.

Others who have maintained their hobbies or found new ones often let them take a back seat to the daily demands of family, home, and work.

There are literally thousands of interest areas and hobbies to be pursued. If old ones are no longer of interest, new ones can be tried. If the new ones are not as enjoyable as was hoped, others can be sought after as alternatives. Winter (1976) states that hobbies can be grouped into four categories offering almost endless choices: doing something, collecting things, learning things, and making things.

Those teachers, administrators, and support personnel who have abandoned former hobbies should make an effort to begin them anew. Hobbies require attention and time and, therefore, take the mind and often the body away from the daily routine. Hobbies are by individual choice and can be pursued at the person's own pace. There are hobbies available to fit almost any time schedule. They can be chosen to fit any budget. Hobbies offer the educator a special form of relaxation and escape from the stresses, tensions, and anxiety of the profession and routine.

Short Vacations

Vacations offer educators a chance to remove themselves from their daily routine and become refreshed. Long vacations are often expensive and require planning. However, short vacations provide an opportunity to "get away from it all," have fun, and relax. A weekend at the beach, one night at a quaint bed-and breakfast inn, or a 2-day romp to an exciting nearby city are but a few of the diversions available to teachers, administrators, and support personnel.

Through use of coupons, group travel arrangements, and weekend travel instead of weekdays when business people flood hotels, short vacations can be enjoyed at relatively low cost. They require little planning. Packing is not too difficult.

Short vacations can be taken whenever needed or desired. After a particularly difficult week, an overnight trip to visit close friends, see new sights, or simply escape to a special place far removed from the world of education is an excellent way to recover and become rejuvenated. There are some people who take short vacations monthly, some more often. Several short vacations throughout the year can be very relaxing.

Time with Friends

Some of the most relaxing times educators have are those periods spent with their close friends. Friends are understanding and appreciative. They share openly and supportively. They offer companionship. Many people converse with their friends differently than they do with spouse and family.

Because of personal and professional schedules, many educators put off spending time visiting with friends. They lose one of the best sources of relaxation and means for stress reduction available. Friends offer so much. And, people have so much to offer their friends. Friendships should be nurtured. There are few things as nice as getting together with close friends to relax and feel good. Taking time to get together with friends should be high on every educator's agenda of things to do.

DEVELOPING A RELAXATION RITUAL

Sehnert (1981) recommends that people develop relaxation rituals. This involves making relaxation a habit. Most educators develop their own combination of relaxation methods and create personal stress-reducing rituals. By developing a routine series of relaxation techniques, an educator can learn to step into a new role—much like an actor does. In stress control, the role the educator assumes is that of an easy-going, relaxed person, not the tense one he or she may be inclined to be.

One technique to help an educator establish a relaxation ritual is identifying daily "pressure" points so that relaxation patterns can be built around them. It is important to focus on those times and incidents that cause the greatest stress and pressure. By taking a brief walk or doing some quiet, deep-breathing exercises during times of greatest stress, extremes of tension and stress can be reduced or avoided. The relaxation resulting from the techniques that the person chooses will have maximum benefit. If, for example, the morning rush of getting ready for work produces stress, then some relaxation techniques should be tried during this period. Making time for a 3- or 4-minute walk, a leisurely look at the morning newspaper for a few minutes, or simply standing outdoors and breathing some fresh morning air before climbing into the car may be helpful.

The relaxation ritual should be based on the relaxation techniques that best suit the individual. What works for one person may not work for another. The relaxation ritual, like any new habit, will require some effort at first. Eventually, it will become a natural part of daily functioning. Sehnert warns, though, that once the ritual is established, a person should avoid becoming so compulsive about it that he or she becomes upset by the inevitable changes that will occur from time to time (Sehnert, 1981).

SUMMARY

Relaxation fights the harmful effects of stress and, therefore, is important to all people. It is particularly important to those who have the greatest difficulty achieving it (Leatz, 1981). When relaxed, people generally feel good. Relaxation affects a person's well-being medically, physically, and emotionally.

Stress causes blood pressure, pulse rate, and other bodily functions to increase. Tension builds as this occurs and people become increasingly frustrated because these physical feelings often seem out of control. It has been shown that relaxation depresses these harmful bodily functions and allows a person to regain equilibrium and a calm state.

There are many relaxation techniques available to people. Educators should select those techniques that best suit their individual needs and schedules. There are numerous books and courses available to people for learning about relaxation techniques.

The relaxation methods outlined in this chapter represent only a few of the relaxation techniques available to people. Some popular techniques include meditation, biofeedback, and other relaxers that require mental imagery and slow, gentle breathing. Pampering techniques are very effective in inducing relaxation. Gentle massage and warm baths are two such techniques.

For some educators, achieving relaxation is difficult. Time constraints and responsibilities of the profession and family seem to interfere with achieving relaxation. Every educator should take time to be alone every day. This may be a few minutes or longer and may be used in any way. Hobbies are a wonderful source of relaxation, but too many people put them off because of other time demands. There are few relaxers better than spending quality time with good friends. They offer a channel for release of stress that is unique.

Every educator should develop a relaxation ritual. It requires making time for relaxation—making it a priority. It involves incorporating some relaxation time into those parts of the day that cause the greatest stress and strain. In also requires developing a philosophy of a more easy-going person. With practice, this becomes natural.

In developing good relaxation habits, it is important for a person to go slowly. Too much too soon, particularly if achieving relaxation has been difficult in the past, could result in discouragement and failure. Practicing a few relaxation techniques until they become habit is effective.

Learning to relax well is similar to mastering any other behavior. Practice is vital. The beauty of relaxation is that the rewards are immediate. The positive reinforcement occurs almost immediately. Stress, strain, and tension are reduced. Relaxation is enjoyable. Comfort, calm, and peace are realized.

REFERENCES

Anderson, R. A. *Stress power*. New York: Human Sciences Press, 1978.
Benson, H. *The relaxation response*. New York: William Morrow and Co., Inc., 1975.
Carnegie, D. *How to stop worrying and start living*. New York: Pocket Books, 1974.
Culligan, M., & Sedlacek, K. *How to kill stress before it kills you*. New York: Grosset & Dunlap, 1976.
Greenberg, S., & Valletutti, P. *Stress and the helping professions*. Baltimore: Paul H. Brookes Publishing Co., 1980.
Leatz, A. *Unwinding*. Englewood Cliffs, NJ: Prentice-Hall, 1981.
McQuade, W., & Aikman, A. *Stress*. New York: E. P. Dutton & Co., 1974.
Sehnert, K. *The family doctor's health tips*. Deephaven, MI: Meadowbrook Press, 1981.

Winter, R. Triumph over tension. New York: Grosset & Dunlap, 1976.
Woolfolk, K., & Richardson, F. *Stress, sanity and survival.* New York: Monarch Publishers, 1978.
Yates, J. E. *Managing stress.* New York: American Management Association, 1979.

Chapter 14

Family, Couple Relationships, and Change

This chapter provides a wide assortment of techniques for coping with stress as it affects family life and couple relationships. It also offers some techniques for coping with change. Some of these techniques can be applied to both work and home life.

For many educators, family and couple relationships often take a back seat to the demands of the profession. As a result, they are not the sources of support that they might be. The educator may feel frustrated because of the time away from family and relationships, adding to work related stress. When these sources of support are strong, stress is easier to manage, change can be addressed, and life seems simpler.

ENHANCING FAMILY LIFE

While stress on the job may, at times, seem insurmountable, it can most easily be reduced if home and family life is tranquil and rewarding. When home offers a positive escape from the work world, strains and tensions tend to flow away quickly. When family is supportive, understanding, and caring, an educator is better able to cope with the demands of the job.

The complexities of home and family abound. Even the model families portrayed on television have their difficulties. When these complexities become too great, external guidance should be sought from friends, counselors, or clergymembers. But, for most educators, following a few basic guidelines can help to make family and home life enjoyable. In turn, coping with stress becomes easier. The time spent in enhancing home and family life is one of the best investments an educator can make. The rewards are many and often last a lifetime.

Following are some guidelines and philosophies for an educator to consider in striving toward a tranquil home life.

1. Admit that the family is less than perfect. Complete peace and harmony is unrealistic. Each member of the family has his or her own personality and, as a result, conflicts are bound to occur. It is important to understand that family members want to belong to one another and be free from one another at the same time. Striking the balance between togetherness and independence is difficult. Most families do so very well, accepting occasional conflicts. It is when the concept of family becomes too idealistic that lifelong disenchantment is experienced.

2. Recognize that money problems can be solved. Financial concerns are at the root of many family difficulties. There are three basic ways to help ease some of the pressures created within the family as a result of finances. 1) Family members should be involved in planning and coping with money matters. All members share the resulting pressure so all should be involved in the planning. 2) Make financial goals family goals. They are more attainable. 3) The financial goals of every family member should be considered in planning budget and money matters. They should be given honest priority in the overall planning.

3. Let quality relationships replace some material things. The values of relationships with family members far outweigh those of consumer goods. All family members will agree that time together in an enjoyable activity is worth more than any new appliance or article of clothing.

4. Let parents have time to meet their own needs. Too many parents ignore or sacrifice these needs. When parents continually subordinate their own needs in the interest of their children, this becomes a major source of stress in the home. Yet, most children are understanding of their parents' need to be together and alone on occasion.

5. An educator should believe in his- or herself and in his or her family members. Doing so is one of the best things an educator can do to spark positivism in the home. Thus, it is important to share this belief. The more confident a person is, the easier it is to deal with stress. Confidence breeds security within the family, too.

6. Reinforce positive behavior. Too often, families emphasize negative issues. The teacher who uses positive reinforcement in the classroom may not use it as frequently at home in relation to family members. Good positive reinforcement habits should be developed within the family. Minimize negative issues that can cause stress; maximize positive issues.

7. Communicate with dialogue. Too often, family members communicate

with monologue, which assumes no participation by other people involved in the conversation. Some people rely more heavily on debate as a form of family communication, which assumes that there will be a winner and a loser. In dialogue, every member of the family participates in the communication and judgments are not passed until all communication is complete.

8. Live from present to future. It is difficult to experience and enjoy the fullness of life if thoughts and feelings remain with the past. Forget what might have been or should have been. A positive outlook toward today and the future should be conveyed to family members. Everyone, including family members, enjoys being with someone who has a positive outlook on life.

9. Maintain consistent guidelines for family operations. The lack of established operating procedures may be stressful to an educator on the job. The lack of operating procedures can also cause similar stress for family members. Designating rules, goals, and reward systems will promote a "smooth-running" family, and such systems will have built-in ways of reducing stress. When people know what to expect and what is expected of them, relationships and willingness to put forth effort are enhanced.

10. Hold family meetings. This allows for discussion of problems before they become serious or explosive. Regardless of the size of the family, regular meetings at which the family's needs are discussed will promote harmony.

11. Avoid comparing family members to others. This is a terrible trap into which many parents and family members fall. When a member of the family is compared to someone else, particularly in a noncomplimentary manner, it demeans his or her individuality and goodness. Feelings are hurt and family harmony is disrupted. Someone will always have more and someone will always have less. To feel positive, a person must first feel good about himself or herself.

12. List elements of pride. It is easy to forget sources of pride and to focus on current concerns. Almost every teacher can point to success stories among former students who might have experienced greater difficulty in school or personal problems had it not been for the interaction and guidance that took place. The same holds true for experiences within the family. On occasion, perhaps during family meetings, members should list the things about which they are most proud as individuals and as a family group. Note the things that distinguish family members from others.

13. Express anger in a constructive manner. Methods should be employed that do not make others angry or cause hurt feelings. One such method is to discuss only the issue at hand and not the individual or personality involved.

14. Learn to deal with anger. Learning to cope with someone else's anger is just as important as expressing anger constructively. This can be accomplished by listening to the person first. Then, clarification of points should

be sought if needed without passing judgment. If the concern is legitimate, compromise may be in order. If not, the opposing point of view should be presented calmly, again dealing solely with the issue and not attacking the other family member.

15. Determine the issues that generate arguments. At a family meeting, the issues that generate most family arguments should be listed. The list of concerns should then be put into priority order, with the most explosive and stressful placed at the bottom of the list. Then, the family should work as a group to resolve the less-heated ones at the top of the list. This provides rapid positive reinforcement to the family's problem-solving efforts. Again, family harmony is enhanced.

Following these 15 steps can lead a family to a more supportive, caring relationship. Tranquility in the home will grow, and the family, which for many people has become a source of stress, can be developed into a wonderful source of stress reduction and personal satisfaction.

COUPLE RELATIONSHIPS

Attention to family is different from attention to a couple relationship. Too many couples confuse them. For parents, married couples without children, or unmarried couples, there are a variety of techniques that can enhance a couple relationship and provide added comfort and enthusiasm to both people involved. A couple relationship can be enhanced by the following actions:

1. Learn to play together and do the things that both people enjoy.
2. Devote time to nurturing the relationship, which may include expressing concerns to one another without fear of rejection, discussing future goals as a couple, and seeking professional counseling assistance if it is needed. Expressing concerns is particularly difficult when both members of the couple are educators, since the sharing may compound rather than relieve existing strain and tension. Caution must be taken to avoid causing excessive additional stress by overemphasizing concerns that are particularly sensitive during times of sharing. Most people can gauge when and when not to share something with their spouse or companion.
3. Date and romance each other. This includes getting ready, making special arrangements, buying flowers, wearing special clothes, and other activities traditionally associated with a date. It requires making time for each other rather than relying solely on spontaneity. Too many couples do not put time into dating one another once they've married. When romancing, it is important to romance a person the way he or she wants to be romanced.
4. Discuss priorities. This requires honest communication about what each person wants from the couple relationship. Time should be set aside for discussing and evaluating the couple's relationship. Priorities to be dis-

cussed may range from what each person expects sexually to taking more frequent walks together in the evening.

5. Establish "free time" periods. Everyone needs time alone, free time away from responsibilities. This time should be provided to one another. Time alone should be supported. But, reasonableness must prevail. The time alone should not interfere with things of importance to the other person.

6. Trade responsibilities. Each member of the couple should experience the other's chores. This can be done on a weekend if a weekday is inconvenient. It is a simple technique that prevents one person from assuming too great a share of the couple's overall responsibilities. This can apply to all members of a family as well.

7. Consider enhancement programs. There are many programs available to couples to provide new insights on relationship. Worldwide Marriage Encounter, community college credit-free courses, and church-sponsored courses are but a few. The information and skills obtained often go beyond the couple relationship and affect relations with students, fellow teachers and administrators, and others.

8. Make master lists. Once goals are established, they should be listed. The list should be kept in a strategic place to serve as a reminder. Similarly, a list of needs, chores, etc. can be developed and placed where it can be seen. This helps to remind each person of what is needed and prevents the other member of the couple from bearing the burden of serving as the couple's conscience.

9. Read. There are many books available that provide helpful hints designed to increase couple closeness.

COPING WITH CHANGE

Change affects all people regardless of age. It is a major stressor in the professional, family, and personal life of most educators. Even positive changes, such as a new home, car, or job, are sources of stress. Drs. Thomas Holmes and Richard Rahe of the University of Washington Medical School, developers of the Social Readjustment Rating Scale, state that change, whether good or bad, causes stress to human beings, making them susceptible to disease (Benson, 1975).

Change within an immediate environment, such as within the home, on the job, or in a couple relationship, has more impact on a person than change in the community. For example, a change in a community's budget or a sudden change in traffic conditions, while having an effect, will not be as significant as a serious family illness, a new supervisor, or a separation. Change is occuring regularly within the American educational system as public and government officials, and the system itself, place greater emphasis on analysis, evaluation, quality of staff, and quality of education in general. The following are some suggestions for coping with the negative or anxiety-producing effects of change.

1. Quality relationships should be cultivated. They allow for discussion of weaknesses, strengths, problems, and solutions.

2. Clubs and organizations offer an opportunity to share with people who have similar interests. This reinforces values and reduces feelings of alienation.

3. A sense of community should be developed. Involvement in community, whether it be in church groups, political groups, youth clubs, or neighborhood or ethnic organizations, offers a chance to become a change agent instead of the target of other people's change. Such participation also provides a sense of stability in the face of life's daily changes.

4. An open mind should be maintained toward change. Despite its inconveniences, all change is not bad. Winter (1976) notes that change can even be beneficial. For example, she encourages change of environment when tension builds up without relief. She also promotes change of routine such as the route traveled to work or the place at which a person shops. In such cases, change offers freshness.

5. Change should be viewed as an opportunity to grow and expand as a person. This requires taxing inner strength to cope. It requires a sense of humor. It requires a positive outlook.

6. Change for the sake of change should be avoided. Many people make changes because they are bored or frustrated, or because other people are changing. There should be valid reasons for change.

7. Change should fit established goals. It is important to have personal, couple, and family goals. They should be listed and reviewed. When this is done, superficial changes become more tolerable because the overall goals are kept in sight.

8. An educator should live according to her or his beliefs. This increases self-esteem and allows a person to cope more effectively with outside influences and controls.

9. Family traditions should be maintained. If they don't exist, they should be started. They provide a sense of foundation no matter how much change takes place.

10. Family and personal heritage should be viewed with pride. These also provide a sense of roots in the face of change. In addition, they increase self-esteem.

11. Loneliness should be met head-on. All teachers, administrators, and support personnel experience some loneliness on a fairly regular basis. They should look upon temporary and short periods of loneliness as a time to get comfortable with themselves. It can be viewed as a positive time rather than a negative, stress-causing one.

12. In the face of change, a person should walk. A walk provides time to think about the change and develop methods of coping with it. It provides a tranquil time to collect thoughts and make judgments.
13. Enjoy change.

SUMMARY

This chapter provides a series of recommendations for enhancing family relationships and couple relationships and for coping with change. If family and couple relationships are good, an educator will better be able to cope with the stresses and strains of the job. The same is true when an educator develops a positive attitude toward change, particularly because of the vast number of changes occurring within the field of education.

No price can be placed on the value of a good family or couple relationship or a positive outlook on the changes that occur in daily life. Any investment made in these areas may reap untold benefits. When family and couple relationships are strong, coping with stress becomes easier.

REFERENCES

Benson, H. *The relaxation response.* New York: William Morrow and Co., 1975.
Winter, R. *Triumph over tension.* New-York: Grosset & Dunlap, 1976.

Chapter 15

Additional Coping Techniques

A variety of additional techniques for coping with and reducing stress are discribed in this chapter. In developing a personal stress-management plan, educators should chose only those techniques that best suit their needs. It is important to remember that stress management rests with the individual. No matter how much stress is caused by an agency, organization, or other people, the individual has the ability to reduce and control it. It requires taking the initiative and assuming responsibility for personal well-being. It requires a decision to move forward toward an improved quality of life.

IN EDUCATION

The field of education is the subject of much discussion among citizens, politicians, and researchers. It seems that every person has some advice to give educators. More discipline, longer hours, shorter summers, more standardized testing, less standardized testing, back to basics, and more formal dress codes are part of the advice being offered. This places additional strain on educators as they seek to cope with stress in the field. The following techniques may prove helpful to educators trying to deal with stress.

Get Enthused about Education

Getting enthused about education is the most general of the ideas offered in this chapter. Yet, its importance cannot be understated. Education is an exciting field. Despite its many stresses and strains, it is an important, dynamic field.

It is difficult for a teacher or administrator who is suffering from job burnout to suddenly grow excited about education. It is important, though, to separate the

151

stresses of a particular school or system from the field of education as a whole. Education remains the basis for the future of the nation. Every teacher, at every grade level, and in every system, shares in preparing today's students to meet tomorrow's demands. On occasion, every educator should take time to reflect on the field of education, its importance, and her or his role in it.

The American School Health Association encourages teachers to maintain a positive attitude and to develop spirit and enthusiasm. Despite the stresses and strains of the job, teachers can take their concerns into their own hands. They are not alone in their efforts to improve their profession and their personal health and well-being (Landsmann, 1978).

Learn Classroom Management

Effective classroom management can make the difference between success and failure before a group of students. It involves preparation and planning, cooperation, positive reinforcement, behavior modification, discipline, and much more. It involves coordinating the classroom and interacting with students to the maximum benefit of everyone involved. It is a skill. It is work.

In their preparation for the profession, many elementary school teachers learned how to effectively manage classrooms. Less attention was given to classroom management for teachers of upper grades, but it is no less important. Classroom management techniques are vital tools for every teacher at every level. They make the difference between an exciting classroom that encourages student growth and a mediocre one in which good enough will do.

John Steinbeck described one of his early teachers.

> She aroused us to shouting, book-waving discussions. We never could stick to . . . the chanted recitation of memorized phyla. Our speculation ranged the world. She breathed curiosity into us so that we brought in facts or truths shielded in our hands like captured butterflies. . . . I have had many teachers who told me soon forgotten facts, but only three who created in me a new thing, a new attitude, a new hunger (quoted in Baughman, 1963).

It is clear that three of Steinbeck's teachers understood effective classroom management techniques. They were able to make their presentations entertaining by putting enthusiasm into their actions and words, thus enhancing classroom management.

There are texts available on the topic of classroom management, and any teacher who wants to reduce stress within the classroom should review them. Additional assistance in classroom management may be obtained from resource centers, conferences and seminars, and other teachers.

Share Information

Teachers are a valuable source of information. Those with experience in managing a class, preparing materials, identifying resources, and coping with problems are priceless treasures of useful data. They can offer invaluable assistance to their peers and co-workers. Too often, educators do not seek information from one another. They allow an exciting resource to go untapped. Seeking aid and information from others can save countless hours of searching and straining to resolve concerns and it provides recognition and reinforcement for the person providing the information.

Seek Commercial Materials

In preparing a lesson or group of lessons, teachers should seek materials prepared by others, whether in the school, the system, or commercial enterprises. These materials can be adapted to fit the teacher's individual needs. By doing this, teachers can save time and energy without jeopardizing quality. With the amount of work facing most teachers each day, almost anything that saves time and energy is worthwhile. An unknown author once said, "Teaching is mostly perspiration in putting a little inspiration to work" (Baughman, 1963). Taking advantage of existing materials reduces some of the perspiration.

Learn to Say "No"

There are many demands made of an educator. One of the best stress reducers available is the word "no." When demands are made and they cannot be met effectively, it is important to say "no." Most people will accept a refusal, particularly when it is supported with a sound explanation. For example, a teacher who is busy tending to classroom matters and is involved in several school and system projects at the same time probably cannot deal with supervising a student teacher or coaching a drama club. When the request is made, the teacher's decline may make the difference between maintaining a manageable workload and losing teaching effectiveness.

Identify Main Goals

Goal planning can reap many benefits. Once the goals are established, educators can use them to evaluate activities by asking, "How does this activity enhance accomplishing my goals?" In preparing a report, for example, it may be worthwhile to avoid complex graphics and charts if the report will not have significant impact on established goals. The time that would go into such graphics and charts is prohibitive. The time can be spent more effectively on a specific, goal-oriented function.

Allow Students to Assist

Some of the stress caused by time constraints and pressures of preparing materials and papers can be reduced by taking advantage of students' talents. For example, students can grade many of their own papers. (Trading papers among students for grading may cause embarrassment and should be avoided.) Allowing pupils to assist demonstrates confidence in the students and provides them with immediate reinforcement as they get rapid feedback on their performance.

Alert Parents to Philosophies

It is useful and rewarding to alert parents (and administrators) to the philosophies that will influence students. Whether it is the teacher's philosophy toward homework or the principal's philosophy on discipline, by informing parents in advance, many problems may be avoided. It serves to create a stronger bond—a team approach—between parents, teachers, and administrators. People work better together when they have a clear understanding of philosophy and goals.

Use Available Resources

When feeling the strain and tension of providing services to students, teachers can turn to a variety of educational resources. Many are provided by state departments of education. Others are provided by local systems. Still others are provided by foundations, private organizations, businesses, and other agencies of government. For example, many states have divisions of instructional television that offer many classroom aids. Police and fire departments in many locales offer programs of instruction according to grade level. Some major corporations have executives who work with schools and teachers to provide an array of programs.

Catalogue Materials

By cataloguing materials, worksheets, and other instructional matter, teachers will be able to meet needs quickly and efficiently year after year.

Make Materials One Size

In designing learning centers, tests, handouts, forms, and other materials, educators should strive to make them one size. By doing so, the materials can be stored and catalogued effectively. When materials are prepared in varying sizes, they may get lost and damaged in storing.

Greet Students

One way to reduce stress in the classroom is to start and end the day on a positive note. By greeting students at the door as they enter, and saying good-bye to them as they leave, a cheerful tone is set. The students respond positively to the teacher's pleasant greeting. It makes them feel special. The teacher reaps the rewards.

Utilize Networking

In recent years, considerable attention has been given to the concept of networking—interacting with others toward mutual goals. In networking, educators grow to appreciate the field and their own school and system, and share this understanding and appreciation with other educators. Networking can be formal or informal. It may involve attending a conference or seminar, or volunteering for a project at the system level. In either case, the educator makes contacts and gets recognition for his or her performance.

Write and Forward Ideas

Many educators have ideas for improving their class, school, or system. But, unless the ideas are thought out, written down, and forwarded, they will accomplish little. In addition to forwarding ideas for improvement through the school or system, educators should send their ideas to those professional journals that print columns of useful suggestions. This wouldn't require the work of preparing an article but would provide the recognition of having an idea published.

Communicate Well

For communication in an educational setting to be effective, it must be honest, complete, and rapid. It requires taking initiative and taking risks. It requires being a good listener as well as a good speaker. It demands that concerns, issues, and suggestions be addressed to the proper people.

John Dewey once said, "Communication is a process of sharing experience until it becomes a common possession. It modifies the disposition of both parties who partake in it" (quoted in Baughman, 1963). The benefits of effective communication are many. The educator who communicates effectively impresses others, eliminates misunderstandings, and opens doors to greater effectiveness.

WINTER'S COPING TECHNIQUES

In her text, *Triumph Over Tension* (1976), Ruth Winter lists 100 ways to relax. Included are a variety of stress-reduction techniques. The following is a summary of some of Winter's suggestions.

1. Don't let things drift.
2. Don't blame others.
3. Do something for others.
4. Make a decision.
5. Do not overdo details.
6. Don't insist on winning.
7. Don't play a role.
8. Compromise.
9. Be healthy.
10. Relax when fatigue sets in.
11. Read a book.
12. Seek humor.
13. Make desires clear.
14. Analyze pet peeves.
15. Do not make excuses.

16. Correct mistakes.
17. Learn to live for today.
18. Be realistic.

Winter emphasizes self-development and self-analysis as two keys in stress management and tension reduction. Other suggestions include:

19. Not allowing things to drift for an extended period of time.
20. Identifying anxieties and fears (Once identified, the process of reducing them becomes easier.)
21. Recognizing that attempts at resolving a problem or issue are failing (Focusing on one problem for too long adds to stress. It is sometimes more effective to move on to the next issue.)
22. Assessing personal views toward winning and achieving (If too much emphasis is placed on winning, stress will increase.)
23. Maintaining a high degree of self-respect (People accept a person's evaluation of himself or herself.)
24. Associating with people who are constructive and supportive.
25. Striking a balance between work and leisure time (Sources of satisfaction should be sought in both) (Winter, 1976).

SOME ADVICE FROM CARNEGIE

Dale Carnegie has long been recognized for motivating people to get the most out of life. In *How To Stop Worrying and Start Living* (1974), he provides suggestions to reduce worry. The process of worrying in itself is stressful. It keeps a person emotionally keyed-up. It does not allow the mind to rest and rejuvenate. It interferes with life's pleasures. Generally, people do not enjoy associating with worriers. Carnegie offers six rules for breaking the worry habit.

1. *Keep busy.* Activity can crowd worry out of the mind. When doing quality tasks, a person provides therapy to the mind. There is little time for worry.
2. *Do not fuss about trifles.* "Life is too short to be little." People should avoid letting little things ruin their life . . . or their day. Carnegie calls the little things "the mere termites of life."
3. *Use the law of averages.* People should use the law of averages to outlaw their worries. This requires that they ask themselves, "What are the odds against this thing happening at all?" If the odds are low, there is no reason to worry. If the odds are high, taking action to address the concern is more effective than worrying about it.
4. *Cooperate with the inevitable.* If a circumstance is beyond a person's control, it is important to revise thinking and accept it. Carnegie encourages that if it is going to be, let it be. Move on to circumstances that can be controlled.

5. *Use "stop-loss" orders.* People should put a "stop-loss" order on their worries. This involves deciding how much anxiety a thing may be worth and then refusing to give it any more.
6. *Let the past bury its dead.* Carnegie says simply, "Don't saw sawdust."

In addition to the six rules, Carnegie encourages a person to:

—Think and act cheerfully, leading to genuine feelings of cheerfulness
—Not waste one minute thinking about people who are not liked
—Count blessings . . . not troubles
—Avoid imitating others . . . enjoy self
—When handed a lemon, make lemonade
—Become interested in others
—Learn to organize, deputize, and supervise
—Solve problems when they occur (do not delay or put them off)
—Keep desks clear, except for the task at hand
—Avoid false crutches and supports (Carnegie, 1974)

In all of his works, Carnegie discourages false supports and encourages people to tackle their lives with enthusiasm and their problems with vigor. Reliance on such supports as coffee, cigarettes, alcohol, and drugs compound rather than relieve stress. Below, some brief suggestions relating to such supports are offered.

Reducing Harmful Intake

Many studies point to the harmful effects of such items as coffee, cigarettes, and alcohol. Yet, many people turn to these items to reduce stress and tension. Their use is often taken for granted. Few people think of eliminating or reducing harmful intake when they consider stress-reduction techniques. Coffee, cigarettes, and alcohol are socially acceptable methods of unwinding. Some people abuse medication and some use illegal drugs as methods of escaping the strains of daily life. Most people recognize the negative effects of illegal drugs and abuse of medication. Often overlooked are the harmful effects of too much caffeine.

Caffeine One cup of coffee contains a minimum of 100 mg of caffeine. People who ingest 250 mg of caffeine can exhibit the same symptoms as those suffering from clinical anxiety. Cigarette smoking has a similar effect since nicotine is a stimulant that causes a person's heart rate to climb (Greenberg & Valletutti, 1980).

Alternatives to coffee and other products that contain caffeine and sugar should be sought. Decaffeinated coffee, herb teas, juice, and club soda are some of the alternatives available to people. If caffeinated coffee is consumed, it should be in small amounts.

Smoking A variety of techniques have been advertised to assist habitual smokers in quitting. Programs are offered by colleges and universities, private organizations, health associations, and public health services. They rely heavily on participants supporting one another. Hypnosis has also been used to assist people in giving up cigarettes.

Drugs and Alcohol Breaking drug and alcohol habits is difficult and generally requires professional and family support. As with caffeine and cigarettes, it requires willpower and a willingness to change on the part of the affected individual. Assistance is available through local health agencies, private and public hospitals, counseling centers, Alcoholics Anonymous, and alcohol and drug abuse treatment centers. Most of these services are offered for free or at a low cost and all information is held confidential.

Religion

The benefits of religion and faith in God have been shown by research to be significant in reducing and controlling stress. People feel better after prayer. An article published by the Religious News Service (Bethany United Methodist Church, 1983), entitled "Going to Church May Be Good for Health," reported that people who attend worship services regularly enjoy physical as well as spiritual health benefits. Dr. Berton Kaplan, Professor of Epidemiology at the University of North Carolina School of Public Health, says studies comparing people who go to church or synagogue services on a weekly basis and those who attend less frequently suggest that regular participation in religious services is good for you.

In a study of 400 residents of Evans County, Georgia, frequent churchgoers were found to have lower blood pressure and therefore are less liable to have a stroke or other physical complications. In a study of about 10,000 municipal workers in Israel, conducted by Dr. Jack Medalie, formerly of Tel Aviv University and now at Case Western Reserve University in Cleveland, workers who infrequently attended synagogue services were found to have a heart disease rate of 58 per thousand, compared with a rate of only 37 per thousand among more religious Jews and only 29 per thousand among the most Orthodox.

Administrative Programs

Programs to aid educators in reducing stress, such as quitting the caffeine and cigarette habits or defeating the effect of alcohol and drugs, can be offered through the school system's administration. The growth, development, and well-being of employees is a primary concern of management. Administrators considering stress-reduction programs for employees will consider such factors as program cost, difficulty in implementation, and the ultimate impact of the programs on the personnel and the agency. Below, descriptions of some of the many programs that the administration of the school system, college, or university may consider as stress-reduction activities are provided.

Administrative Education For stress-management programs to be successful, they must first be understood and supported by administrators. Any effort to improve the system or school as a whole should begin with top-level administrative personnel. It enhances the credibility of the program.

Mid-Management Education Because of their role in providing direct daily supervision to staff, it is essential that mid-level managers receive instruction in stress management and control. As with top-level administrators, such an effort will add credibility to the program and demonstrate a genuine interest in the topic.

Staff Education Staff education should provide a general overview as well as some immediate reduction techniques. It should be offered on a regular basis, updating information and encouraging participation. Classes, sessions, or meetings should be held at convenient times and should be led by dynamic instructors. The entire system will benefit as a result.

Coordination with Employees' Organizations Since the administration and the employees' organizations (whether they be a union, fraternal group, or team of teachers from the same grade level or subject area) serve faculty and staff, their cooperative effort in stress-management programs will increase chances for success. Too often, the employees' organizations are overlooked in implementing stress-management programs. In some systems, the administration and employees' organizations have duplicated efforts in stress management instead of working cooperatively toward a mutual goal, the well-being of educators.

Career Development Alternatives Programs that provide career development alternatives demonstrate an interest in the employee from the time he or she enters the field until and after retirement. For instance, career enhancement programs serve to reduce stress and burnout and provide recognition and incentives to employees. This may be done through salary incentive programs, authorization of additional responsibilities based on merit, provision of opportunities for highly specialized skills development for teachers and administrators, and implementation of an effective quarterly (or more frequent) evaluation system. The primary purpose is to assist the educator in developing his or her potential to the maximum throughout an entire career, not simply during the early formative stages.

The effectiveness of career educators is at the foundation of the educational system. As L. A. Morrill stated:

> There is an exaggerated notion at the moment, especially at the secondary level, that curriculum reform is the be-all and end-all of our difficulties, with a seeming forgetfulness of the fact that the curriculum is but an educational instrument of small significance except as it derives integrity and strength and effect from the capacity of the teacher to instruct and inspire (quoted in Baughman, 1963).

Counseling Services Counseling services may include financial counseling, personal and family counseling, career counseling, vocational counseling (as part of the career development effort), and pre-retirement counseling. They can be obtained through local health agencies, colleges and universities, and private services. Counseling services offered to employees should be confidential and accessible.

Family Orientation Programs   Family orientation programs are educational programs that orient the spouse, children, parents, and friends of teachers, administrators, and staff to the nature of the school. Those who participate become familiar with the school's philosophies and goals, teaching techniques, problems experienced by educators, stress-management programs, and more. They then become a stronger support group to the educator, and gain a better understanding of the educational process and the role of their family member in it.

Phased-Retirement Programs   Relatively new, phased-retirement programs involve easing a person into retirement so that the shock of leaving a position of responsibility does not become overwhelming. During this period, in which the person works less and less during his or her final years, new skills or recreational pursuits are taught. The system helps the practitioner prepare for retirement over an extended period of time.

Exchange Programs   Few things make a person feel better about his or her school or agency than seeing someone else's organization. The grass is not always greener. Exchange programs offer an opportunity for employees to learn new skills, share with new people, and gain new experiences. They can be arranged among schools within the same locale or system, or between different systems.

Health Care and Physical Development Programs   Programs designed to improve health care and physical development include after-school courses in nutrition, or exercise programs before classes begin, during lunch, or after hours. They may also include physical health screening, which may range from simple eye, ear, and blood pressure testing by the local health department, to detailed physical exams by a physician. Every member of the educational system (e.g., administrators, teachers, support personnel, students, and parents) benefits when teachers and school administrators retain their health. In many systems, existing medical benefit programs, such as Blue Cross and Blue Shield or other health maintenance organizations, provide some funding and organizational support to such programs. Employees' organizations often encourage them.

Role of Administration

There are many other programs that should be considered by administrators in implementing stress-management activities. In doing so, input from every personnel group should be sought. It is clearly the responsibility of administration to support and encourage personnel at every level to perform to their maximum. It is the responsibility of administration to take steps toward improving the well-being of employees. It is the responsibility of administration to encourage participation of employees in helping the system to grow and achieve its potential.

The benefit of a cooperative effort toward implementing stress-management programs is improved services to students and more satisfied employees.

SUMMARY

There are many techniques for coping with and reducing stress. It is up to each person to develop a stress-management program applying the techniques that best meet his or her needs. Each individual must assume responsibility for his or her own stress management. Implementing a stress-management plan requires initiative and a decision to have an improved quality of life.

In education, a number of techniques can be applied to reduce stress in the classroom. Educators at every level should become familiar with classroom management. Other techniques range from utilizing students' skills in such activities as grading papers, to making educational philosophies known to parents.

Ruth Winter provides a variety of practical stress-management techniques in her text on reducing tension. Her advice includes such approaches as seeking humor, maintaining self-respect, and avoiding placing blame on other people. In all, she offers 100 suggestions in her text.

Dale Carnegie encourages people to take control of their lives and stop worrying. Worry, he notes, is a drain on energy and time and prevents a person from relaxing and coping with stress in more positive ways. He suggests that people weigh the amount of time they spend on worrying about problems against the worth of the problem itself. Most people will find that the issue is rarely worth the worry. The worry itself accomplishes little.

A part of any stress-reduction effort should be reducing or eliminating intake of harmful products such as coffee and other caffeinated products, cigarettes, alcohol, and drugs. Some of these induce anxiety-like symptoms and all compound daily stresses and strains. Programs exist within the community to assist in overcoming smoking, alcohol, and drug habits and abuses.

Religion and faith in God offer excellent outlets for stress. Research shows that people who participate in church services on a regular basis are less likely to have a heart attack. They are also less likely to have high blood pressure.

There are many administrative programs that can be implemented to aid employees in reducing and controlling stress. They include educational programs for administrators, mid-managers, and all staff members. They also include counseling services for employees, phased-retirement programs, and family orientation programs. Any program implemented by administration should involve input from employees at every level of the organization or agency.

REFERENCES

Baughman, M. D. *Educator's handbook of stories, quotes, and humor*. Englewood Cliffs, NJ: Prentice-Hall, 1963.

Bethany United Methodist Church. *Going to church may be good for health.* Charlotte, NC: Religious News Service, 1983.

Carnegie, D. *How to stop worrying and start living.* New York: Pocket Books, 1974.

Greenberg, S. F., & Valletutti, P. J. *Stress and the helping professions.* Baltimore: Paul H. Brookes Publishing Co., 1980.

Landsmann, L. Is teaching hazardous to your health? *Today's Education,* April/May, 1978, 49–50.

Winter, R. *Triumph over tension.* New York: Grosset & Dunlap, 1976.

Chapter 16

Conclusions
and Implications

Stress is silent and subtle. It sneaks up on an educator and causes or compounds illness and disease before he or she realizes what has happened. Stress can be harmful when its negative effects continue unchecked for too long a period. It has been linked to such disorders as headaches, backaches, stomach problems, spastic colon, fatigue, insomnia, sexual difficulties, skin rashes, and many others. It has recently been cited as a factor in the growth of cancer.

Stress exists in the field of education. It is unlikely that anyone in the field who assumes responsibility for the well-being and growth of students has not experienced the negative effects of stress. The tasks to be performed by educators and administrators are growing more complex, placing additional burdens on educators at every level. The field of education is being scrutinized more closely than ever. Commissions and task forces make recommendations for change that affect every member of the educational system.

The work of the helping professions is difficult. Rewards are often few and not highly visible. Pressures are great. Situations regularly occur calling for ingenuity, innovation, and diligence. The human service professional entered his or her profession with visions of a supportive institution staffed with effective supervisors and administrators and cooperative patients, students, or clients. He or she anticipated making a difference in people's lives. What he or she found instead was red tape, harried supervisors and administrators, and an unreasonable workload. No one has prepared her or him for this. No one comes forward to help him or her cope with feelings of inadequacy and frustration. If the worker is looking for a great deal of personal fulfillment, she or he may quickly grow frustrated and begin to burn out (Freudenberger, 1980).

Despite the stresses, strains, tension, overwork, and burnout experienced by

163

many people in the field, education remains one of the most exciting and important professions in modern society. Even though daily routines take precedence in the classroom, every educator has the opportunity to affect and guide students. This opportunity may be spread over an entire school year or may be as brief as a single class or a single meeting in an office. Few other professions offer this opportunity. The dilemma between wanting to teach and serve students and functioning within the often straining environment of the educational system is a primary source of stress to many educators.

INDIVIDUAL INITIATIVE

Many people who work in a stressful environment wait. They wait for the agency or a supervisor or a friend to resolve the stress and strain that exist. They gripe to others about how bad the situation is but do little to improve it.

Combating stress requires *initiative*. It requires assuming *responsibility* for personal well-being and for a bright, healthy, enjoyable future. It requires *work* and *commitment*.

Combating stress is not difficult. It does not require a great amount of time. It does not require great amounts of money. It does not have to involve other people. Nor must it have to include a rigid schedule of activities or a lengthy list of tasks to be performed.

Combating stress is up to the individual. Every educator must assume responsibility for her or his own stress management. A personal stress-management plan should be developed, choosing from the suggestions offered in this text, from the many available in book stores and libraries, or from information obtained from classes, physicians, counselors, and friends.

Almost every educator will have to break some old habits and create new ones. These may focus on dieting, exercise, learning to relax, or developing new goals and attitudes toward the profession. Changing habits is not easy, but it is possible. It may require assistance from others or may simply require applying principles of behavior modification to one's self. Focusing on stress in other people's lives is one of the first habits that many people will have to break. If stress is to be reduced and controlled, the focus of attention will have to be on one's own stressors.

It is also important for the individual to focus on realistic stress-management goals. Many educators face a myriad of stressors every day. To attempt to reduce and manage all of them or a large number of them simultaneously is building failure into the plan. Stress management should be approached like a fine lesson plan, establishing clear, realistic goals and incorporating all of the support and planning necessary to make it work well.

Yates (1979) notes:

Stress can be bad enough when you are dealing with just a few stressors at a time, but you are probably actually facing multiple stressors in your life. This complexity resulting from multiple stressors makes it absolutely necessary for you to approach stress management with the broadest of perspectives, integrating stress reduction insights and techniques into your life and making the appropriate reinforcing behavioral, psychological, and physical changes. To do any less is to be applying bandaids when tourniquets are needed.

MAKE THE PLAN FIT WELL

The individual stress-management plan should be tailored to fit like a glove. This may require experimentation with stress-reduction techniques. At first, the techniques tried may be disappointing. Some require continued use over a period of time, such as self-hypnosis or meditation. Others, such as strenuous physical exercise, offer immediate rewards. A trial-and-error approach and experimentation will be required of most educators in the beginning stages of their effort.

The most effective management or organization plan for an educator's daily life, time, or money is one based on her or his personal values, goals, priorities, needs, and resources. Only the individual can create such a plan. It requires an investment of time and effort, but the results are worthwhile. The plan can always be altered, or even scrapped entirely if it no longer meets your needs (Leatz, 1981).

IMPLICATIONS FOR THE SCHOOL SYSTEM

It has been estimated that stress costs between $10 billion and $20 billion annually in lost work days, minor illnesses and injuries, hospitalization, and early stress-related deaths (Sehnert, 1981). This does not include losses due to lowered employee effectiveness. It also does not reflect the loss of experience when a teacher with 5, 10, or 15 years of service leaves the system, Quality experience is priceless.

The expanded study of stress is relatively new. While Selye and others have been doing research on the subject for many years, it is only within the past 5–10 years that business, industry, and government have given attention to the effects of stress on their personnel (Greenberg & Valletutti, 1980). In some businesses and industries, inservice training for employees, medical screening and physical development programs, relaxation breaks, vacation scheduling based on seniority, and phased-retirement programs are just a few of the activities underway. Business and industry place a high value on experienced, dedicated, happy employees. Employees with positive attitudes and dedication to the firm equate with higher productivity and ultimately increased profits. Everyone benefits, from the entry-level clerk to the chairperson of the board of directors.

THE STRESS-MANAGEMENT TEAM

In government, stress-management programs are just beginning. While the individual must assume responsibility for the management of stress in his or her own life, the administration of an agency, educational system, college, or school also has a responsibility to provide assistance to employees. One of the best ways in which administrators can meet this obligation is to have classroom practitioners, mid-managers, and top-level managers function as a stress-management team. Their combined efforts will surpass anything that could be accomplished individually.

The stress-management team should begin by identifying key stressors within the educational system and at specific grade levels, resources areas, or school districts. Each member of the team will bring his or her own perspective to this process. The team should provide careful analysis of the stressors, soliciting input from as many levels of workers as possible, including teachers, clerical personnel, resources and support personnel, and management. Then, the team should analyze the alternatives and programs available to address the stressors, choosing the best available alternatives. The team should oversee the implementation programs and provide evaluation reports to top administrators. Then, the team should make periodic reviews to identify new or recurring stressors and provide recommendations for resolution.

There are many benefits to a stress-management team in an educational system. It provides input from various levels within the system. It allows for development of programs to deal with stress that will be of greater value because they reflect this input. Furthermore, the team approach will help to reduce the "us versus them" attitude that causes failure in so many administration-dictated programs. The team identifies problems, concerns, and issues while they are small. This saves the administration headaches and money. It is always better to address a source of stress in its early stages. The team also allows for enhanced communications between administrators, mid-managers, and classroom teachers.

ADMINISTRATION'S ENCOURAGEMENT

The administration of the school or educational system should encourage employees to use effective stress-management strategies. Administrators should openly push employees toward good health. They should implement programs designed to support positive attitudes and encourage continued dedication. Such encouragement is humanistic and inexpensive (Yates, 1979). If enough people respond, the entire system benefits. There are fewer losses due to illness. Fewer educators will use sick leave because of mental and emotional exhaustion. There will be less turnover. More positive attitudes will be reflected in the classroom and among co-workers. Everyone, in particular the students, benefits. In short, administration's involvement in promoting stress management makes good sense. The success of any stress-management program will be contingent upon proper planning, involvement of all levels of the work group, and a logically formulated evaluation model (Greenberg & Valletutti, 1980). In the final analysis, participation in the programs rests with the individual.

In a relatively short time, stress-management programs will exist in every system and in almost every college, university, and school. College students majoring in education will take courses on the subject to prepare them more realistically for what is ahead. An individual who is prepared to cope with the stresses and strains of the job is better able to plan, implement, and evaluate tasks. She or he will approach the job more realistically and will respect his or her own limitations as well as the limitations of the system. He or she will communicate more freely and openly and will have a more positive attitude. Home and personal life support rather than conflict with professional life. The opposite is also true as professional life enhances personal and family life rather than interferes with it. The individual will better meet the commitment to students, helping them to learn, seek, and grow—the foundation of education. The philosopher Plato wrote, "A good education consists of giving to the body and the soul all of the beauty and all of the perfection of which they are capable."

REFERENCES

Freudenberger, H. J. *Burnout: The high cost of achievement.* Garden City, NY: Anchor Press, 1980.

Greenberg, S. F., & Valletutti, P. J. *Stress and the helping professions.* Baltimore: Paul H. Brookes Publishing Co., 1980.

Leatz, C. A. *Unwinding: How to turn stress into positive energy.* Englewood Cliffs, NJ: Prentice-Hall Inc., 1981.

Sehnert, K. W. *The family doctor's health tips.* Deephaven, MN: Meadowbrook Press, 1981.

Yates, J. E. *Managing stress.* New York: American Management Association, 1979.

Suggested Readings

Anderson, L., & Van Dyke, L. *Secondary school administration*. New York: Houghton Mifflin Co., 1972.

Benjamin, B. E. *Are you tense?* New York: Pantheon Books, 1978.

Benson, H. *The relaxation response*. New York: William Morrow and Co., 1975.

Bright, D. *Creative relaxation*. New York: Harcourt Brace Jovanovich, 1979.

Carruthers, M. *The western way of death*. New York: Pantheon Books, 1974.

Cooper, C. L. *Understanding executive stress*. New York: PBI, 1977.

Culligan, M., & Sedlacek, K. *How to kill stress before it kills you*. New York: Grosset & Dunlap, 1976.

Dean, M. C. *The stress foodbook*. Washington, DC: Acropolis Books, 1982.

Dowdell, D., & Dowdell, J. *Your career in teaching*. New York: Julian Messner, 1975.

Forbes, R. *Life stress*. Garden City, NY: Doubleday, 1979.

Friedman, M., & Rosenman, R. *Type "A" behavior and your heart*. Greenwich, CT: Fawcett Publications, Inc., 1974.

Galton, L. *The complete medical, fitness, and health guide for men*. New York: Simon & Schuster, 1979.

Girdano, D., & Everly, G. *Controlling stress and tension*. Englewood Cliffs, NJ: Prentice-Hall, 1979.

Goldberg, P. *Executive health*. New York: McGraw-Hill Book Co., 1978.

Graham-Bonnalie, F. E. *A doctor's guide to living with stress*. New York: Drake Publishers, 1972.

Greenberg, S. F., & Valletutti, P. J. *Stress and the helping professions*. Baltimore: Paul H. Brookes Publishing Co., 1980.

Heald, J. E., & Morse, S. *The teacher and administrative relationships in school systems*. New York: Macmillian Publishing Co., 1968.

Jacobson, E. *You must relax*. New York: McGraw-Hill Book Co., 1976.

Katch, F., McArdle, W., & Boylan, B. *Getting in shape*. Boston: Houghton Mifflin Co., 1979.

Kinzer, N. S. *Stress and the American woman*. New York: Anchor Press/Doubleday, 1979.

Leatz, C. A. *Unwinding*. Englewood Cliffs, NJ: Prentice-Hall, 1981.

McQuade, W. *Stress*. New York: E. P. Dutton & Co., 1974.

McQuade, W., & Aikman, A. *Stress*. New York: McGraw-Hill Book Co., 1974.

Madders, J. *Stress and relaxation*. New York: Arco Publishers, 1979.

Mitchell, L. *Simple relaxation.* New York: Atheum, 1979.

Morse, D. *Stress for success.* New York: VanNostrand Rienhold Co., 1979.

Morse, D. *Women under stress.* New York: VanNostrand Reinhold Co., 1982.

Pelletier, K. R. *Mind as healer, mind as slayer.* New York: Delacorte Press, 1977.

Pembrook, L. *How to beat fatigue.* Garden City, NY: Doubleday, 1975.

Ringer, R. J. *Looking out for #1.* New York: Fawcett Crest, 1977.

Selye, H. *Stress without distress.* Philadelphia: J. B. Lippincott, 1974.

Selye, H. *The stress of life.* New York: McGraw-Hill Book Co., 1976.

Shaffer, M. *Life after stress.* New York: Plenum Publishing Corp., 1982.

Steincrohn, P. J. *Questions and answers about nerves, tension, and fatigue.* New York: Hawthorne Books, 1978.

Straus, R. A. *Strategic self hypnosis.* Englewood Cliffs, NJ: Prentice-Hall, 1982.

Tanner, O. *Stress.* New York: Time-Life Books, 1976.

Tressider, J. *Feel younger, live longer.* Chicago: Rand-McNally, 1977.

Winter, R. *Triumph over tension.* New York: Grosset & Dunlap, 1976.

Woolfolk, R., & Richardson, F. *Stress, sanity, and survival.* New York: Monarch, 1978.

Yates, J. E. *Managing stress.* New York: American Management Association, 1979.

Index